The Tribal Reign and Autonomous State Failure

Changkuoth Gem Panyuan

The Tribal Reign and Autonomous State Failure

DEDICATION

In matter of fact, it's all about that you went losing your lives in senseless meant. This book is dedicated to all innocent civilians who lost their dear lives on the 15th of December 2013 onward in unknown political setup from political elites. Make sure that your people know what, why, how and who killed you. As you know, the South Sudan you were fighting for as well as you all expected to be your country in equal basis became different since you were killed by your own people in mid-December. But make sure that the accountability should be claims on those who led perished your lives in eyes of your children, wives, husbands and communities. And the due legal process should be following only a matter of time. Dedicated to all separatist leaders and strong men of South Sudan who's their sacrifice bring the independent South Sudan of today. The country you expected peaceful co-existence fall short into another civil war when the tribal driven politics rocked the country in hand of SPLM.

The children, wives, communities and the whole country you were fighting for has been plunged into senseless tribal killing by your comrade in struggle. We know that you do work hard for this country. But you have gone together with your vision and talented leadership style. The few individuals who try to follow your foot step are those becoming victimized in today's South Sudan. If dead can see, hear and talk, we hope you can have some to says to these comrades "Rest in Peace".

LISTS OF ACRONYM

AMISOM: African Union Mission in Somalia

AU: African Union

AUCCISS: African Union Commission for Crime Investigation in South Sudan

BNFA: Bentiu, Nasir, Fangak, Akobo

CCM: Chama Cha Mapinduz

CEWARN: Conflict Early Warning

C-I-C: Commander In Chief

CID: Criminal Investigation Department

CoH: Cessation of Hostilities

COMESA: Common Market for Eastern and Southern Africa

CPA I: Comprehensive Peace Agreement

CPA II: Compromise Peace Agreement

CPMR: Conflict Prevention Management and Resolution

G-7, 10, 14: SPLM Former Detainees Group of Seven, Ten and Fourteen

GRECOR: Great Equatoria Council of Rights

GRSS: Government of Republic of South Sudan

IDPs: Internal Displaced Persons

IGAD: Intergovernmental Authority on Development

IGADD: Intergovernmental Authority on Drought and Development

IGASOM: Inter-governmental authority on Development Peace and Support Mission in Somalia

IGP: Inspector General of Police

INSA: Information Network Security Agency

J1: Presidential Palace in Juba

JCE: Jieng Council of Elder

JEM: Justice and Equality Movement

MVM: Monitoring and Verification Mechanism

NGOs: Non-Governmental Organizations

NIF: National Islamic Front

NLC: National Liberation Council

NUP: National Union Party

PB: Polite Bureau

PoWs: Prisoner of Wars

SPLM/A: Sudan People Liberation Movement/Army

SPLM/A IG: Sudan People Liberation Movement/Army In Government

SPLM/A IO: Sudan People Liberation Movement/Army In opposition

SPLM DC: Sudan People Liberation Movement Democratic Change

SRSG: Special Representative to Secretary General

SSDF: South Sudan Defense Force

SSIM/A: South Sudan Independent Movement/Army

SSLM/A: South Sudan Liberation Movement/Army

SSTV: South Sudan Television

TGoNU: Transitional Government of National Unity

UDSF: United Democratic Salvation Front

UN: United Nation

UNMISS: United Nation Mission In South Sudan

UPDF: Ugandan People Defense Force

ACKNOWLEDGMENTS

World is full of up and down, but with some very important individuals around you, it may become a plate leveled ground in every circumstance. First, I would like to thanks my creator for his guidance throughout this all routs. Secondly, I have thanks all my family, friends and contributors to this finding for their firmly stand on what become the success of this task. Of course, I have thanks all my friends and relatives both abroad and at home for their standing behind me in this life test where they stand as role model and a comedian of day to day drama making my days reasonable for research. Guys, your intervention and encouragement are what make this piece of cake today, "if not, I can't". In fact, the situation that I faced during finding may force me to skip the work but your words keep me doing it. You guys know that I couldn't manage to collect enough words for your thanksgiving in connection to your tireless advising approach you have assists me throughout this study. You already know that you have helped me today, tomorrow and even next tomorrow. Anyways, stay blesses!

FOREWORD

Good administrative direction is masterminded by active citizenship. Dormant citizens have nothing to do with change either in government or community level. The author of this book calls the citizens of South Sudan to know their task and responsibilities in their country both from government and in their respective communities, to exercise their role in meaningful and convincible manner which can bring together all the nation, nationalities and people of the Republic of South Sudan. Author of this book entitled, "The Tribal Reign and Autonomous State Failure" calls all the ordinary citizens, youths, elders and political leaders to eradicate tribalism which is the main cause and driving forces of every misunderstanding among South Sudanese. Tribalism is the only Satan and longtime stayed evil spirit which has grown inside some South Sudanese leaders especially from two largest tribes of this country "Nuer and Dinka".

Nuer and Dinka most of the times were the opponent who like to run up for the leadership position. This leadership position struggle carries with it an intension which is also reflected in government system. This describes South Sudan political arena and governmental system as the traditional way of leading the nation. Tribalism is what result in Nuer ethnic and other minorities cleansing since December 15, 2013 in capital Juba and nowadays in every corner of South Sudan.

It is unfortunate for political debate to be turned into civilians cleansing based on ethnic line by the elected official of the country. The leaders of South Sudan need to adopt and understand the fruit of democracy as the only mean for conflict resolution. The government needs to open space for its citizens to exercise their right as per constitutional directive. Citizens' participation in government system is the only source of change and rout to unity.

Good citizenship is made not born. To make good citizens, leaders are the responsible tools to help secure safe environment for citizens' participation. Good leadership stage is show by statesmanship. Being statesman require forgiveness and toleration. Political tolerance is the only mean to compromise and the helpful way to get rid of perfectly leading the nation. State failure, meant carelessness for civil right. This is based in the absence of security, health, humanitarian service and so on. Collective hands of citizens and governing body are the only mean for state existing.

PREFACE

December 15, 2013, the first day when innocent civilians were massacred in capital Juba is marked a black day of South Sudanese, especially Nuer ethnic group around the globe. It was the first day in which blood of innocent civilians from Nuer and other minorities started bleeding in the land which God has given them to live in. What escalated to massacre was said to be political debate between politicians of SPLM ruling party. This resulted into massacre of Nuer ethnic group in capital Juba and sparked losses of more lives, destruction and targeted killing based on tribes. The citizens of South Sudan left empty handed when country was plunged into civil war by their own elected leader.

The tribal division along ethnic line was what triggered more hatred against ethnic groups which resulted into more different massacre apart from Juba massacre. Targeting of Nuer ethnic group in capital was what resulted into Nuer white army revenge for the sacks of their beloved one. Below is the letter of white army fighter who learns with great dismay the death of his mother, two sisters and their uncles killed in Juba and their bodies were dumped into mass grave. Dear mother, this morning I will be leaving for Paloch, a key oil-field in the very heart of Upper-Nile. Machar told us that closing of oil will force Kiir to stop bringing more Ugandan that fuels the war. And maybe we shall "REALIZE PEACE IN OUR NATION".

However, I know you were already gone and my two sisters in Juba. So, I am not fighting for Machar but for the freedom of your daughter in Kakuma camp who have been there since independent. If you were not killed and my uncles in Juba, today I could be doing my final exams in Ethiopia by the end of this year. Something I wish you could be proud of, but now you are gone. This will be my third letter since I came from Gambella.

And in each battle, I decide to be writing to you in spirit until we defeated the enemy who threatened to wipe us out of this great land which God of heaven gave to us. I heard you were burnt alive somewhere I have never seen in Juba; Muniki block 10 alongside many innocent civilians of Nuer who knows nothing about politics. But hours from now we shall win the victory of Paloch. Mom, I dedicated this battle to your loving memories. I will come to Juba through God almighty power and see the mass grave that your ashes were dumped in. we are strong here and victory is certain.

The world closed its eyes to see our suffering and guns I am using I got it from the battle field we fought last month in the town of Malakal in which for the first time in my life I saw river of blood and thousands dying. Therefore, I have courage that I am committed with hope that we shall defeat the evil and bring peace to the entire South Sudan and freedom. Your loving son, he concluded. It is unfortunate and surprising as well that the ever-political debate from country's leading politicians turned into ethnic cleansing by the same elected officials in the country.

South Sudanese people were senselessly killed by their government before the general election of their country was conducted. The election of 2010 was republic of Sudan's general election not South Sudan. The author, as a concerned human has experiences of how good your home is different from other countries and does not want anything like this happen to this young nation. The author respectfully calls the commitment of South Sudanese leaders and people particularly elders to come together, to discusses and tackle whatever an obstacle which can obstruct this compromise peace agreement (CPA II) brokered by IGAD head of states.

This can let the orphans, displaced civilians, and general population of South Sudan comes back to their home, and to live in harmony like what they expected during signature of CPA I in 2005. Southern Sudanese are the same citizens of the same country having the same human and democratic right in equal basis. This book is valuable because it briefly discusses the causes of the massacre categorized in to main and immediate cause each with its own chapter. It also discusses all the history of rivalry, between Nuer and Dinka as the two large ethnic groups in South Sudan. This rivalry was started before Anglo-Egyptian condominium rule.

The story of rivalry between these two tribes since then is discusses starting from the first fallout in the years before colonial power; liberation struggle of 1955 (Torit Mutiny); the two Anyanya movements of 1963-1983; the formation of SPLM/SPLA in 1983; the split of 1991 and the Khartoum peace accord of 1997.

The SPLM/SPLA re-unifications in 2002 and the defection of what is now the president of the Republic of South Sudan Salva Kiir Mayardit, the CPA of 2005 and the massacre of Nuer civilians in December 2013 are also briefly discuss inside this book.

As the country was known for its liberation history, it's also known that within every liberation struggle of South Sudanese people, the split is massive supported by tribalism which is the top agenda inside some of the South Sudanese leaders. With the help of this book, the author hope that South Sudanese would come together and correct the backwardness and differences which still grasp back this country. The author challenges the leadership system of SPLM party in which some of politicians demand its reform. The author criticizes it starting from their decisions of giving political position based on file and rank of SPLA rather than political potential which someone can afford to lead the nation.

How can a military leader experience the ways of handling thing through politic when holding the political post? Nevertheless, the answer is to say by order (talimat in Arabic) like what is in the army and later becomes the dictatorship tendency [which is termed as decree in politic]. Decree by itself is the fruit of dictatorial leadership. The decree to be issue by the president of the country is limited based on country's constitution, and if there is anything that needs to be decreed by executive order, it should be approved first in parliament. When there is no approval from parliament as well as there is no limitation in constitution, this kind of executive decree is fruit of dictatorship seeds.

Decreeing is not in good governance system, because what to decree is almost not found in the constitution. And it is reasonable ground would be to state it by strong authoritative words of president or other powerful bodies within the government and should be implemented. The author can appreciate if the leaders of South Sudan make creation of more federal state with clear demarcation zone (borders) their top priority, for South Sudanese to witness the decentralized and Federal Republic of South Sudan where long term lobbied development could be achieved as well as human and democratic right should be exercises. So, the mode of this nation, nationalities and people should be restored.

We have got to keep matching

In many ways success for self-determination is the culmination of action from August of 1955-2005. South Sudanese were on the dawn of the new days and it had taken daylight a long time to come. The essence of 1947 South Sudanese leaders' speech for demand of federation was not the dream rather it was broken promise. South Sudanese also have been promised the accommodation of full citizenship, which is the right to vote. We have been promised equal protection and equal opportunity under the law, yet in our quest for citizenship the promise has been broken.

The spirit at the struggle was that we were winning and we were doing it together as Nuer and Dinka as well as other South Sudanese. We were multiracial and social-justice coalition that was before we had the public accommodation and before we had the right to vote but those victories were in vain.

We had this sense that we were winning, we were rising and we had to overcome fear. These speeches were early indications that if we keep matching and pushing surely, we are going to win this battle. It was a dawn to daylight speech and we won. Now, we had the sense that we are at dusk, moving toward midnight. One thing we can recall from Anyanya II leaders' speech is that the force of equal protection should neither sleep nor slumber. We got the right to vote in 2010 after 49 years of humiliation from North but in 2013, the supreme SPLM leadership chaired by President Salva Kiir eviscerated it. The struggle for democracy and equal protection will never be a past-tense discussion, though **"we have got to keep matching"**

Dream of democracy

When Dr. Martin Luther king gave his speech ''I have a dream", he must have known that few people believed such a vision could become true. Nevertheless, he did not hesitate to stand up and speak. Throughout history, idealists have been willing to commit to dreams that seem impossible but the dream is more powerful than violence.

Do you see when tank rolled in street of capital Juba where dozens of innocent civilians were killed? Most people are now in exile but I know our hope for democratic South Sudan will eventually be realized. History allowed Martin Luther king's dream to prevail, and then **'' South Sudan also deserves to dream"**

Lastly, as the writer have starts it with this piece of cake, more ideas in written form to help us are going to come soon and this title (writer) is going to be kept.

Your support for this book is more appreciated and valued as well. This book will let you; the author and everyone in our communities understand the backwardness we have. It would enable everyone who understands its contents to correct this backwardness and find reasonable ground for the way forward. If so, I hope this book is going to guide you.

Table of Contents

Chapter One

An Existed Tribal Motive Behind December 15, 2013 Massacre

The causes of December 15, 2013 massacre were derived from many evidenced sources of data and known experience which everyone has ever witnessed. They included the poor and traditional politics derived from tribalism, lobbying for political posts, widely used corruption and the plan for building one man ruled autocratic state of South Sudan. But the most influenced one is the old age rivalry between Nuer and Dinka as the two large ethnics group in South Sudan. This rivalry was historically caused by tribalism and was also brought into governmental system of South Sudan. This is what has contributed bitterly to the failure of this country. The placing of South Sudan in the failed states list in 2014 is not the only outcome of this tribalism exercised in governmental system. This tribalism has a lot of consequences since it has destroyed and caused a lot of lives, properties and other failures. Draw back to the period of preceding liberation struggle since the two Anyanya movements, tribalism played a great role in destroying the nations, let alone the writing of South Sudan as a failed state in 2014 was the minor consequence during this period.

When we look deeply into period of Anyanya (1963-1983), the tribalism is what contributed mostly into failure that caused those movements not to struggle for one united heart; instead, they were looking for who dominated what. The tribalism did not only affect the two Anyanya movements but also became the top agenda of some South Sudanese politicians during formation SPLM/A. The disagreement between Anyanya II and SPLM leaders in 1983 was the result of tribal motive behind their agendas. Dr. John Garang, a member of SPLM/A opposed the proposal of Anyanya II leaders for his uncle Kuot Atem to become chairman and commander in chief of the movement.

The reason behind this rejection was that Kuot Atem was not well known from Dinka communities and insisted that Dinka will suffer under his leadership This was where the bitter division occurred which led to war between liberators and unifiers. This war resulted in loss of lives of great leaders from Anyanya II in which the man described as charismatic, smart and most intelligent military leader General Gai Tut from Nuer was killed by Dr. John Garang's ordered soldiers in Thiajak (Adura).

Dr. John Garang was from Dinka ethnic group and his action of ordering soldiers to kill General Gai Tut was the worst cause of war which lasted for about four years between Gai's Anyanya led faction and SPLA which were about to be emerged as a one movement. It is also the same tribalism that has brought the unrest of today's crisis which was started as the political debate between politicians of the SPLM ruling party.

These politicians were tribally driven by hatred which has resulted in killing of Nuer innocent civilians and now rock the whole country as the civil war. These causes can be defined in many ways but were contained in two divisions for simplicity of understanding. These divisions are categorized as main causes and immediate causes, and are discusses differently. What are categorized as the main causes of December 15, 2013 massacre, have briefly crossed whatever the history of South Sudan since the day of declaration for popular demand which was federalism in 1947.

The tribalism which some of Southern Sudanese politicians has practiced more than anyone's expectation, is also discussed. This practiced tribalism has contributed well to the failure of previous movements. Although the agreement that led South Sudanese to won the heart of international community in period of 2005 which resulted in signature of CPA have been also discuss. It is known to everyone that if those hatred, tribalism and traditional politics did not become the main practice of South Sudanese; the liberation movement could get its head before 2005. This book also briefly discusses the rivalry between Nuer and Dinka as the two large ethnics group in South Sudan. This rivalry has a lot of negative effect on whatever became the liberation movement of South Sudanese. To be more understandable, the briefing is carried out on stages of liberation struggle and the negative contribution of tribalism is filed out.

1.1 The Old Age Rivalry Between Nuer and Dinka As the Two Large Ethnic Groups in South Sudan

The old age rivalry between Nuer and Dinka was started long ago when communities were under the control of traditional tribal leaders, and the prophets who tasked themselves for protecting their communities. Nevertheless, those differences were not about the political misunderstanding. They were only due to the needs for grazing ground of their animals because domestic animals and agriculture are backbone of South Sudan economy since the time they were in village.

The communities of South Sudan involved in some conflict but resolved in traditional basis. Those tribal rivalries between Southerners due to grazing ground were between Nuer and Dinka, Tapossa and Dinka, Murle and Nuer, Dinka and Murle, Shilluk and Nuer, Shilluk and Dinka, Anyuak and Nuer and so on. But those differences were solved based on traditional ways of solving conflicts. The conflict between Nuer and Dinka became the bitterer one which claimed a lot of individuals' lives. A lot of people claimed that this conflict was started during the rise of Prophet Ngundeng Bong from Nuer ethnic group.

Nevertheless, this conflict was started before the period of prophet Ngundeng. This conflict was said to have started during the Nuer expansion movement from western Nuer in Bentiu (Nuer home-land) to eastern Nuer, the present day of Lou and Jikany Nuer land.

On their way from Bentiu, Nuer were moving in more number, took with them the belonging of other ethnic group they have got along their route, for example livestock. They also took with them the girls of those other tribes for example Shilluk, Chay (Maban), Munduk (Uduk) and Dinka. The other cause was their taking away the land of other tribes because the land in Latjor area was said to have been annexed from Dinka, Anyuak, Chay and Munduk while the present day of Lou Nuer land was said to have taken from Murle, Dinka and Anyuak. Other sources claimed that the land nowadays occupies by Lou and Jikany Nuer were not the habitats to any human being before they have settled there. Those claims have not been verified by the author.

The author's analysis fall short of that the areas were vast empty territory for the first time but with expansion of Nuer after they have settled, some lands from the other tribes were taken. Due to the above cases, Nuer was condemned by those neighboring tribes, so that the war of robbery and revenge were fought based on tribe. Some years later, after Nuer had settled, Longoar and Nuer-mer rose as prophets. These men were alleged to have historically come from Dinka ethnic group, came to Nuer land and have tortured Nuer ethnic group in what was said to be indirect revenge killing. Longoar was the man who builds houses with the people.

He built the foundation with short men and roof with tall men. After some days, these people must die being tied up constructed. This torture was practiced on Nuer by Longoar. In other hand were Nuer-mer and his group who also carried out unwanted activities on Nuer.

Nuermer always sat down under the shade of big tree near the main route that the people used to move. When he saw a person, he used to start a debate by saying what is in stomach of that person? What did him/she eat? Some might say Wal-wal, some said Kop (the most dominant Nuer traditional food) and other said Milk. After those answers, have given, he must order his men. He should order them to see what is inside stomach of that person. His guards were to ripped open the stomach of the person as ordered and the people were dying day by day based on that matter. Those actions were alleged to have being practiced by Dinka doom prophets on Nuer ethnic group which was also fueling up the relationship failure between these two tribes. Due to these all misbehaving behavior, the war between Nuer and Dinka became continued war without end.

Some years later, Ngundeng Bong and Luang Chaak rose as prophets both from Nuer and Dinka respectively. These two prophets were in competition for protecting their communities. Ngundeng was in Waat where his Bie was situated. Luang Chaak was a Dinka from Luach section. As the robbery and tribal relationship deteriorations growth, the conflict was still growing up between these two tribes. One upon a time, Prophet Luang Chaak started to mobilize the Dinka youth of Luach section to fight prophet Ngundeng of Nuer. As the war broke out, overseeing Nuer ethnic group, Prophet Ngundeng Bong picked up his rod and shakes it to prophet Luang and his fighters. Because of that shaking, the rod of prophet Ngundeng has exploded and killed all the fighters of Luang Chaak including prophet Luang himself in Pading.

This battle was called Pading battle remembered for great loss from Luach section as well as the day that the rod of prophet Ngundeng was broken. All those Luach fighters and other Dinka clan mobilized for war against Nuer were dead without a single person being survived. The hatred against Nuer became developing when this news had reached Dinka communities and Nuer negativity toward Dinka was also increasing. So, the conflict was still coming up in worthiest form.

After a while, British had colonized Egypt and extended its colony to Sudan in which south was a part of that colony. A British man who wrote the scripture of prophet Ngundeng was there as a close friend to Ngundeng. This white man was given a Nuer name as Kolang Jiar Kuach because it was hard at that time to pronounce white men's name, the only easy way to know them was to create them a name by local language. Kolang was the very best British friend to Prophet Ngundeng Bong at that time. Before death of prophet Ngundeng, Kolang Jiar Kuach was shifted to central government in Khartoum by administrative order and served there. Some years later, prophet Ngundeng die and his position was occupied by his son Guek Ngundeng.

At that time, another prophet from Dinka Nyarweng section raised up, this man was called Deng Malual. Prophet Deng Malual was still unhappy for what was happened to his tribal men during Ngundeng period. Due to this, he went to Khartoum and had a consultation talks with Kolang Jiar Kuach telling him that Ngundeng has died and he was succeeded by his son called Guek Ngundeng, now the prophet's son is waiting you for war saying Nuer land become free from British rule.

Kolang was convinced by Malual's words and told Malual to help him fight the war with Guek "the son of Ngundeng" and then he had agreed. Kolang armed Malual's fighters and his force, and then the war was ordered against Guek. When the war broke out, Guek Ngundeng was killed and the prophet's resident was destroyed in central Waat where his Bieh was constructed. As the result, rod (Dang), drum, Tuokding and Tony-lang of prophet Ngundeng were taken to Khartoum and then to British by Kolang Jiar Kuach.

The British force that joined hands with Deng Malual was called "Turuk Deng Malual" in Nuer Language; meaning government of Deng Malual. After some years, the fruitful news of peace agreement between Nuer and British colony were circulated and their relationship was restored. As the result of that peace agreement, Nuer was promised by British colonial government to be governed based on their cultural law. For the implementation of an agreement, British government wrote the Fangak document (distuur Fangak in Arabic) "a constitutional document". This Fangak document was all about the bylaw of Nuer ethnic group and their historical ways of living like custom, norm and the culture which were incorporated to be respected. As of this agreement, the British colonial administration that govern Nuer was administering them based on Nuer cultural law written in Fangak document up to their exit in Sudan. The conflict between these two tribes continued up to total exit of British from Sudan in 1954.

Traditional peace initiatives were signed between these two tribes but were violated by tribal motives. In 1952, Egypt withdrawn from Anglo-Egyptian condominium rule and the question for independent Sudan was raised. British agreed to give independent to Sudan but the debate between Sudanese regarding British exit from Southern part rocked the Sudanese parliament at that moments. The debate was between Southern and Northern representatives in the Legislative Assembly. The Southern representatives were worried about their provincial development where they didn't see a single strategy for development. This idea was supported by all the thirteen representatives of South. To present their grievance, they adopted a minute of petition represented to British administrators by Abdel Rahman Sule, a trader in Juba and co-founder of the Liberal Party, before the first sit of new cabinets in offices. The petition stated that:

No one in South would be convinced to see this Egyptian proposal carried out successfully in Sudan. We in the South are still undeveloped economically, socially and politically. If the Egyptian proposal to deprive us of our safeguards vested in the Governor-General is accepted, we ask Your Excellency that there will be no any other ways for us except to ask for federation with the North. Failing to federate, we shall ask as an alternative for the appointment of a High Commissioner from the British Foreign Office to Administer the South under the Trusteeship of the United Nations till such time as we shall be able to decide our own future.

The problem was that British was fully convinced to give away the independent of Sudan, so there was none to act on favor of Southern question. On other hand were also the Southern tribal caucuses who were politicized by National Union Party (NUP) and Egyptian parties' agreement where the Southern representatives were excluded. Those groups were supporting the idea that British must exit from Sudan including Southern part and we should have left in Sudan as Sudanese people. The reason behind those tribal caucuses was the idea opposition against those representatives in legislative assembly. Some groups were citing the reason that we were Sudanese even before British colonialism, for that reason ''we don't have any ground to claim our loneliness as South Sudanese out of Sudan''.

On other hand were groups sometime in line with the representatives' claim. They were saying that British must wait in South Sudan for twenty years. These groups were citing the lack of education, health center and leadership in South and they need British to open school, build hospital and teach people for leadership etc. Those groups were formed when the Southern representatives exaggerated the need for federation. Some of these groups status was acting against the appointment of Senator Stanislaus Paysama, the Vice-President of the Liberal Party, who hail from Bar el gazhel and was chosen to explain the meaning of federation.

On other hand were groups who acted jealously about the role played by John Both Diu, a Nuer who responded and withdrawn the target question of Necodimos Gore.

Necodemos Gore raised a different question from all the attender, he asked that: In case we receive Federation, where shall we get the people to run it? How are we going to Finance it?" John Both Diu responded him with a very strong worded response:

May I draw your attention all the attender present in this house? He asked. I want to know whether you in this house want to be slaves or it will be better for you to be Free and happy. As it was explained to you by senator Paysama, federation does not mean separation but internal Law and order in the united Sudan. It's for you to be able to look after your own affairs. My brother Necodimos Gore brought the question of management and finance of the Federation. Regarding your question, the present Government must be bound to manage the federation of South for fear of separation, if they cannot we can manage to separate the country. In conclusion, he said to Mr. Gore that: my brother we are here for freedom not for money. This answer drawback the attention of those who did not fully understood the exact meaning of federation.

The role played by John Both Diu based on his action sparked a lot of allegation some claiming that the task that was given to Senator Stanislaus Paysama was taken by John Both. So, the tribal reaction between the supporters became growing but everyone left the room having in mind the real meaning of federation. After all, the solution to legislative assembly debate and the Southern question was given a chance to conduct a referendum. The referendum was conducted, and those who demanded the British exit from Sudan as whole won the pool.

During this referendum, Sudanese government in Khartoum was supporting the idea of British exit as whole in Sudan. They released a full fund of money used to bribes the Southerners who opposed the idea. This was where the word "kith" in Nuer was formulated. Because in that referendum, there was a little white sack filled with coins and stacks which were estimated to be one thousand and were given to one person as a bribe. This was where the word "kith" was derived which meant full sack of one thousand money. When the result was declared, Benjamin Lwoki President of the Liberal Party, Abdel Rahman Sule chairman of the Juba branch, John Both Diu from the House of Representatives, the Senator Paulo Logali Wani from Equatoria and Stanislaus Paysama from Bahr al-Ghazal, accepted the result but said we must find our own government from north.

This remark was documented by those British colonial administrators who chaired the meeting. When South Sudanese jointed Bush in 1955 in protest of humiliation by North, British have admitted it that this was what Southern leaders said during our exit and the solution to this would be giving South Sudan its independent. The debate that engaged federates and unionist on British exit in Sudan was turned into Bar el ghazel group and Upper Nile group each having its own agendas. Each of this group carried with it a tribally motivated agenda against the other one. The differences pushed by tribal motivation were on ground exercised even during the start of liberation struggle when the first mutineers protest in Torit, 1955.

The tribalism that was brought into politics started to appear badly in liberation movements of Anyanya I, Anyanya II and SPLM/SPLA. It became more complicated when taken into leadership system since formation of SPLM/SPLA in 1983. The old age rivalry was also a driving force which facilitated the split of 1991 and then the massacre of innocent Nuer civilians in December 2013. Those differences, taken on tribal basis by politicians were what resulted negatively on South Sudanese civil populations. The tribalism is the causes to every chaos in South Sudan due to the mishandling and lack of leadership Potential.

1.1.1 The Torit Mutiny of 1955

South Sudanese were struggling for recognition since the early age of British exit in Sudan. The popular demand by South Sudanese and others marginalized societies of Sudan in 1947 were not given a priority to be an exercised one but as a highlight to make thing calms. It became a plan for South Sudanese to only wage a war of liberation against aggressors after Khartoum government's failure to equalize Sudanese right before the law. On August 18, 1955, the rebellion broke out as a mutiny and was called a non-commanded mutiny.

Nevertheless, it was said to have commanded by the second lieutenants identified as Ronaldo Loleya, Commander Emilio Tafeng, Ali Gbattala, Fr. Saturlino Ohure and comrade Akwon along with others prominent leaders. This mutiny broke out due to many reasons in which the demand for recognized South Sudan was the leading objective.

The mutiny was started as a simple misunderstanding in the army. That misunderstanding was said to be the resistance on order from central government, in which the southern military platoon commanded by the second lieutenant Ronaldo was told to be transferred to north and serve there. But the fact about South Sudanese now of 1954-55 was that they were in move for self-recognition. That was why they refused to be transferred and served under north to give a service which was their tasked obligation. They waged an unexpected war of liberation in Torit when they were told to leave immediately as ordered by central government in Khartoum.

During this period, South Sudanese participated well and only looking for independent South Sudan without tribal domination and influence. But some months later, little differences started to rise. Some of them were for leadership and some were for domination of movement. Of courses, this movement was dominated by Equatoria (Lotuko, Bari, Madi, Acholi, Zandi), Nuer, Shilluk and others. Meanwhile they were those above mentioned ethnic groups having dominated a lot of officers' positions in the movement. This domination caused differences in which some tribes were against each other but the real competition was between Dinka and Equatoria and on other hand, it was between Dinka and Nuer. Those differences grew internally and forced the movement's leadership to look for other ways fearing the failure may erupt on tribal basis.

Since the leadership of movement feared the internal wrangling may causes failure and loss of objective, the movement's leaders left with no company at all but to accept the dialogue which demanded the recognized South Sudan within Sudan government. This idea was developed when the movement was approached for negotiation by Khartoum government. Some months later, the peace initiative was kicked off. As per negotiation, the leadership accepted to go back and serve under Khartoum government being promised some right and were hoping that the agreement would be respected. Nevertheless, the northern Arab dominated government was really a true aggressor who didn't want South Sudan to be recognized. In a very few months after peace initiative, Chairman, 2nd lieutenant Ronaldo Loleya ended up being killed in fired Squad while his other comrades who were estimated to 300 were killed in cool blood.

Imagine! If South Sudanese were still uniting themselves like how the movement was started, do you think they could not won their objective through struggle? The answer is no! They could win. This is because if the struggle continues with one tied heart, the decision to accept dialogue could not be given a priority, if not, the agreement might not be mistreated like what was happened. Due to that mistake where South Sudanese could regret a lot and learn a lesson, none of the leaders has paid great attention and still pursued their way of tribal politic which only leads to the loss of individual's lives up to this stage So, the living condition in hand of Khartoum government became challenging.

The unlawful detention and cool blood killing on mutineers was rising day by day. And then, the next step became the formation of new movement while the powerful men already perished.

1.1.2 The Anyanya I Liberation Struggle (1963-1974)

The struggle for South Sudanese rights to be recognized did not ceased due to unfortunate death of great leaders like Ronaldo Loleya and his comrades who were mostly killed in tortured manner of fired squad. The new movement was formed having well and qualified military leaders like Paul Awel, Paul Ruot Wichluoth, Agrey Jaden, Gordon Muortot Mayian, Joseph Lagu, and others. Those who served in Anyanya I liberation movement were mostly the remnant of Torit mutineers in which their experience has something better on how the movement's objective could be carried out.

During their first phase as a fresh guerrilla fighting forces, everything went smoothly. Thus, very successful wars were waged against oppressors that led to the down fall of military regime of General Ibrahim Abboub in Sudan. The name Anyanya was called after a name of snake poison from Bari language, a tribe in South Sudan's Equatoria ethnic group of central Equatoria Region. The movement's name was referred to that snake poison as its logic related the Anyanya liberation movement to be a poison to government in Sudan.

During that time, all South Sudanese were very happy and highly motivated. Their talk is all about, "we are fighting for just causes and everybody hope for one heart to guide South Sudanese liberators and give a solution to the marginalization in Sudan".

Yes! The movement went like what was expected and became active from period of 1967-1969 where many operations became successful under command-ship of Aggrey Jaden. Even if, Anyanya I was relatively strong, it was also affected by internal wrangling between its leading politicians, in which the tribalism was a driving factor. Anyanya I liberation movement was mostly dominated by Nuer ethnic group followed by Equatoria, Shilluk, Anyuak and less from Dinka. The internal struggle between politicians on lobbying for position and difference in opinions and strategy brought about another misunderstanding which resulted in further failure.

In 1969, this internal struggle for leadership position led to decision by leader comrade Aggrey Jaden to abandon the movement leadership due to frustration with lack of cohesiveness and bickering within liberation movement. Shortly after Aggrey left, Gordon Muortot Mayian was endorsed as a leader of the movement and appointed Joseph Lagu as his chief of general staffs. The operations which were carried out under Muortot and Joseph Lagu were more successful where many battles were fought and succeeded in defeating the enemy. Nevertheless, internal struggle derived by tribal motive did not stop there. The need for leadership by some Dinka politicians rocked the movement in which they dotted the movement's positional flow as it was between Nuer and Equatoria.

The struggle went on with this internal rivalry being cool down by the administration. But some years later, chief of generals' staff Joseph Lagu started to jointed hands with chairman's opponent mostly from Dinka ethnic group and started to plan a coup.

Before the coup was attempted, Joseph Lagu negotiated with Israel where the movement's army equipment was supplied. His point of negotiations is to divert the arms they supplied for the movement to him and carryout his coup plan against chairman Muortot. What triggered the coup was claimed to be the movement's name "South Sudan provisional government" was changed into "Nile provisional government" under Gordon Muortot. Joseph Lagu criticized this name as it only concerned the great Upper Nile region in which the name excluded Bar el gazel and Equatoria region. Others opposed sources to Lagu's reason cited from different authors claimed that; this was a made-up claim because no one can say, "I want to take over power on my own will, without being approved by movement's leadership".

Joseph Lagu was just in need of leading not because of that name change and this was how politics was going. In politics, if your opponent derives a plan which you thought may be resists by some party; you may take bold position to get supporters. Of course, Joseph Lagu got supporters and carried out his coup attempt plan. He was pushed by a belief that he is the only powerful commander in the movement. As Joseph Lagu and his comrades ran up the deal, he attempted his coup in 1971 by toppling Muortot from power.

Gordon Muortot who jointed bush to liberate his people from Arab dominated government, gave the power peacefully and continued with struggle as high-profile comrade like others. Lagu assumed the leadership of the movement and became strong both politically and militarily by waging deadly wars against northern government. Instead of Nile Provisional Government under Muortot, the name was changed to South Sudan Liberation Movement/Army (SSLM/A). In 1972, Joseph Lagu saw opponents from his own comrades who helped him took over power from Muortot. Lagu thought that the same coup might be carried against him. Fearing that something might happen, Joseph Lagu agreed on peace talk with Khartoum government. This peace talk was coordinated by Sudan council of churches and was mediated by emperor Haileselasie of Ethiopia.

The known fact was that Lagu did not submit the movement, instead he and his comrades negotiated well by promising the implementation of the agreement signed by the two parties. Addis Ababa peace Agreement which was mediated by Ethiopian Emperor Haileselasie was signed to end 17-years civil war. This agreement was first rejected by some of the leading commanders including Immanuel Abuur, and other within the movement. However, a letter circulated to all Anyanya force which detailed the position of rebellion against the peace agreement was intercepted.

Southerners were given rights to exercise per agreement except in area of finance, defense, foreign affair, social and economic planning and inter-regional concern.

These are the authorities to be handled by national government in Khartoum. The signing date of Addis Ababa peace agreement was celebrated as a national Unity Day in Sudan. For the sake of peace, President Jaffer Nimeiri issued a decreed putting the agreement in position. But due to influence of Islamic affairs that Khartoum want to impose, the Khartoum government violated the peace agreement by imposing non-agreed laws, for example, Sharia law and other non-agreed northern political agenda on South.

As peace agreement was signed, the struggle for position of Southern regional leader became the main issues. Joseph Lagu and his chief negotiator Philip Pidak Lieth were excluded from the southern regional governor position by the group of politicians who were inside during the struggle. This group was led by Abel Alier. Their excuse was that the movement was dominated by Nuer and Equatoria. This decision led to serious disagreement between Joseph Lagu and Abel. Abel Alier was not in bush together with Joseph Lagu, instead he signed a setup deal with Jaffer Nimeiri that switched Joseph Lagu for the regional position.

Abel ALier agreed with president Nimeiri and disapproved some demand of Southerner signed in agreement by the two parties. Nimeiri has other interest in South Sudan's Upper Nile in which he thought he would be successful by placing the great Upper Nile son in that position. Abel Alier was a son of Upper Nile, secondly, he accepted the "Nile canal" to be built by Nimieri, and then Nimeiri gave the position to Abel.

This created a bitter conflict between Joseph Lagu and Abel Alier which gave Jaffer Nimeiri a chance to play mind game on South Sudanese. As the Southern government was established, Abel Alier was appointed regional governor and Peter Gatkuoth Gual was appointed deputy. Gai Tut was appointed minister of wildlife; Joseph Lagu and Daniel Koak Guok were put in charge of army. When the ministers started works in their respective ministries, Samuel Gai Tut, a wildlife minister imported guns from Uganda and gave them to wildlife service men. When Abel Alier heard this, he wrote a letter to Nimieri that Samuel Gai imported guns and wanted to defect against our government. By presidential order, Nimeiri dismissed Samuel Gai from ministerial post and told Abel to nominate his position.

For the case of nomination, Abel Alier called his right-hand men from Dinka which included his Justice advisor Martin Majiar Gai. He suggested to them that he want to appoint Joshua Dey Weng Kor, a commissioner of Al anil at that time. All the men conformed to his suggestion but his Justice advisor told him that it's better to appoint another person rather than Dey Weng.

His reason was that Dey Weng would be going to correct the structure of state government because the entire secretariats were given to Dinka. He said it's better to leave Dey Weng in his commissioner post and appoint another person. But Abel resisted saying that he knew Dey Weng very well when they were served as one party members in Khartoum. After their meeting, Dey Weng was called minister of wildlife in state and within that week, Abel went to workshop out of the country.

Joshua started the work in his ministry by reshuffling all the employees. He dismissed all the secretariats and reappointed some; mixed them with new faces from Nuer and Equatoria. He presented the new structure of his ministry to deputy governor Peter Gatkuoth who was also delegated by Abel in suit of governor. Peter Gatkuoth signed the structure and those all dismissed Dinka were left without being employed. As of this structure, the dismissed Dinka employees wrote a letter to Abel that your government was took behind you by Nuer. Some days later, Abel came back from workshop and urgently called a meeting between him and Dey witnessed by Peter Gatkuoth Because of this meeting, Governor Abel Alier dismissed the signed structure from Dey's ministry and for that reason, the disagreement had occurred.

Within three days, Nuer called their general meeting where all Nuer government employees including deputy governor Peter Gatkuoth wrote a letter of resignation having undersigned their names in protest of what has been done by the governor.

After the resignation letter was summited, the governor forwards it to central government in Khartoum. The government of Nimeiri discussed the issue and has known that Southern government had got a problem. During this meeting, the security organs acknowledged it that the new rebellion led by Nuer has been formed and established their base in Bilpham. If we are going to exclude Nuer from this government they would joint their fellows in bush. The decision to re-structured Southern government in to three regions was made to be the solution to that misunderstanding.

Southern government was divided into three regions made up of Al a-nil with capital in Malakal, Bar el gazel with capital in Wau, Equatoria with capital in Juba. These three regions were appointed their three governors in which governor Abel Alier was excluded. Abel Alier hailed from Bor community of Dinka ethnic group in Al a-nil. He hoped that he might be shifted from his position to Al a-nil governorship but central government in Khartoum changed its mind. The new appointment has reached a Nuer man called Daniel Koat Duoth. After Abel Alier has learned of new development, he called a meeting in his home and alerted his community that they were excluded from the government.

At that time, John Garang was colonel in army as well as he was an educated. Abel Alier told John Garang to go to bush in which he assured him that the government in bush would be the government that might bear fruit. He told John Garang to form another movement that can fight for unified Sudan. Abel also promised John Garang not to give chance again to Nuer and Equatoria who always dominated us as long you became educated and a military leader. Abel Alier convinced at least seven military colonels together with John Garang to support each other and should assume leadership of the rebel movement by any mean possible. So, their community would benefit. That was what resulted into John Garang's defection where he fought Anyany II faction for leadership purpose in Itang. After all the Khartoum government, has learned that South Sudanese disagreed, Nimeiri declared the imposition of laws which were also a violation to signed peace agreement.

The harsh treatment reoccurred in claims of that south Sudanese rebelled against Khartoum government. You see! The tribalism was what made Southerners missed all the chances signed in agreement and gave an opportunity to oppressor which his only objective is to torture Southerners. President Nimeiri became exercised without caring of signed agreement. At that time comrades in the South who wanted to see their people in equal treatment before the law had left with no other decision but to wage another war of liberation against north. The other war of liberation struggles re-started three years later in 1975 which is what became Anyanya II liberation movements and was followed by group of defectors in 1983 where SPLM/A was formed.

1.1.3 The Anyanya II Liberation Movement and formation of Sudan People Liberation Movements/ Army (SPLM/A) 1975-1983

When South Sudanese discovered the deception of northern government, they decided again to take arm for another liberation struggle. This plan had been in process since 1974 and broke out as a mutiny in Akoba 1975. A sergeant who helped narrated this part was there as guard to Vincent Kuany Latjor and some years later became aid to Gen. Simon Gatwech Dual. He explained:[1] When mutiny broke out, every one of us was informed of what was going to happened.

---

[1] Veterans of Anyanya two, some of them became retirees from SPLA narrated the history confidentially when reached by author in SPLA IO held territory. A guard of Benson Kuany Latjor and one of the secretariat of Koang Chuol in Bilpham were among the contributors.

At that time, Vincent Kuany and Gordon Koang Chuol communicated and told us that there were high ranking military officers who would come from north; therefore, none us should put their orders in action. A brave young man with name James Bol Kur was given an order to stand in-front of armory and was told not to let anybody open the armory except Vincent Kuany. When those officers came, they were not received by any commander including Kuany and had walked up to armory. After their arrival at armory, the young man did not salute the officers. They ordered the young man based on military rule but the man refused to give an attention of respect to the officers. A high-ranking officer came directly to the guard to confirm what the man meant because saluting is the military rule which mean respecting seniority and military conduct.

But instead of penetrating into 0.5 meters, the man shot the officer on his head and this became the starting point of the mutiny. As it became the liberation movement, Vincent Kuany Latjor was nominated the leader and the name of that movement became Anyanya II which carried the same style from Anyanya I liberation struggle. Few months later, the movement was joined by a lot of defectors from Equatoria, Bar-el-gazel and war continued against northern government. In 1982 many soldiers together with Samuel Gai Tut, Abdalla Chuol Deng, Kuot Atem and other comrades defected from north and joined the movement. Those were very important men who experienced a lot in military as well as having a God given leadership talent.

At that time, the movement became more active and the first mutineers became more courageous knowing that their effort was not in vain. Some months later in 1983, a bunch of army from two battalion of Miya arbaa (104) and Miya kamsaa (105) commanded by William Nyuon Bany defected from Ayod, while another powerful commander called Kerbino Kuanyin Bol from Bor defected with his soldiers and joined the movement. Kerbino who was personally wounded during his defection was assisted by a captain from Miya sabaa (107) in Pibor called Kir Tang Kier up to Bilpham.

Within May of the same year 1983, Dr. John Garang defected, citing humiliation from Khartoum government and joined the movement in Bilpham. Dr. John with his promised objective in mind was most educated among the other while Samuel Gai was more experienced military leader. Their arrival opened another chapter of reshuffling the ranks and file of rebel movement. This calls for reshuffling was resisted by some individuals from the Anyanya II former comrades because those new arriving comrades did not respect the Anyanya leadership.

The comrades in Anyanya II were ignored due to their low education achievement only having two Bachelor degrees, University dropout, Diploma and some high school certificates. Most of Anyanya II comrades were both uneducated and narrowly supplied with military equipment like ammunition, bullets and other. Due to the needs for presence of strong movement, Anyanya II leaders compromised and gave peace a chance and accepted a call for new leadership structure.

Samuel Gai and his group including Abdalla Chuol, Kuot Atem, Lokurnyang Lado, Gatjiak Wieh and others, demanded priority for Anyanya II leaders. They called for their respect because they were already in bush for the first time. All Anyanya II comrades led by Samuel Gai were separatists who wanted the foot step of Anyanya I to be followed. John Garang and his group including William Nyuon Bany, Kerbino Kuanyin Bol, Arok Thon Arok, Salva Kiir and other comrades came up with idea of changing the movement's name and objective. This changing of the movement's name and objective carried with it the promise of Abel Alier to Garang but Nuer on John Garang's side do not know anything regarding that secret.

They proposed the Sudan People Liberation Movement with military wing as Army (SPLM/A) to be a name of the liberation movement in which its objective should be uniting Sudan. But this name and objective were opposed by many of the leaders who said the name Anyanya was historical. Nevertheless, Samuel Gai advised them to accept it and went on with one objective as well as united liberation movement. Really! Formation of SPLM/A in 1983 was the hardest part of the history where true tribally derived politics was exercised between Nuer and Dinka.

Misunderstanding between Anyanya II and SPLM/A was caused by tribal motive and it has added fuel into fire as the tribal conflict between these two tribes was historical. The immediate point of disagreement was the proposal on leadership.

As Samuel Gai believed in seniority, he proposed Kuot Atem, the uncle of John Garang to be chairman of the movement and the army. Samuel Gai proposed himself a commander in chief of the army and John Garang as chief of general staff. But John Garang declined to accept the proposal and he secretly disseminated the news to Dinka fellow that; "Uncle Kuot Atem was not a man aspiring to lead. One and for most, Uncle Atem was very weak both politically and militarily. He was also not popular in Dinka community and he was not capable to lead the movement as he lacked both political and military capacity to carry out the tasks.

All responsibilities and leadership would go to Nuer and that of Anyanya I and II would repeat itself, so Dinka would suffer". He suggested this idea to Kerbino Kuanyin Bol that Dinka would suffer under Uncle Kuot's leadership and Samuel Gai was going to take over all the work and the movement should be dominated by Nuer again like in both Anyanya I and II. John Garang convinced his group to reject the proposal and his hidden agenda of lobbying for position by himself and his promise was not circulated to Nuer who were together with him. Though, they had rejected the proposal of Samuel Gai and his group. John Garang was asked to present his proposal in which he could offer whatever option that could be good for the new movement. He gave his proposal by proposing Samuel Gai as chairman of the movement and army. He proposed himself commander in chief of the army and appointed his right-hand man Kerbino Kuanyin Bol as chief of general staff.

But Samuel Gai and his group who included former Anyanya leaders rejected the proposal and discovered the mind game John Garang was trying to play. A secretary of Gordon Koang Chuol at that time summed up the story for one day conversation in his resident. The secretary who was there during the split narrated;

What Garang tried to do was direct tribalism. None of us expected it to happen from a senior and well educated leader like him. It was not only a direct humiliation against Nuer tribe but also to South Sudanese in general, we totally rejected it.

What intensified the problem also came from Garang because instead of coming together with other leaders and talk about how to handle this misunderstanding, he located his base in Makot (Itang). Garang signed a deal with Ethiopian government of Mengistu Hailemariam and got the fund with ammunition, so he did not want any more to talk with us. Gai who needed one united movement of South Sudanese told us again to go to Makot in Itang and have a talk again with Garang.

Instead of negotiation, Garang came out with his army under Nyuon Bany holding their machine gun and surrounded us but we were told by our commanders Koang Chuol and Gai not to escape even a single meter. At that time, William Nyuon did not start any shooting but he told us to go back to Bilpam and have talk with our commanders only.

Vincent Kuany did neither joint any discussion between us and Garang nor came to Makot. Gai planned to delegate some comrades who could be left behind in Itang to talk with Garang and his group about the matter. At that time, Koang Chuol rejected to remain in Itang for talk with Garang. But Gai and Abdalla chuol whom they always called Dhalla chuol delegated some comrades' other than Koang to remain there for discussion. Instead of discussing on what should be the structures of the movement, John Garang jailed those delegated comrades in his base. Those delegated comrades who were jailed included captain Kir Tang Kier who helped assisted Kerbino and they were very important men from the side of Anyanya II faction.

Eeeh! Eeeh! When this information reached us early in the morning in Bilpham, we whistled our whispers and started matching toward Itang having our gun in hands together with all our leaders. Our leaders talked to them on speedy move while misunderstanding was still imminent. He released some of our comrades and retained two important educated men with him whom he killed later. The comrades he has retained and killed later were captain Kir Tang Kier and Doctor Gatwech Khan. At that time, Samuel Gai and Abdalla Chuol talked to us seriously with tear up to ground saying; 'we are going to fight these people and their leader John Garang". Within that day, the decision to leave Bilpham was taken by our leaders while some other comrades including myself were sent to Nasir for resource mobilization.

Other men were sent to Bilpham to inform Vincent Kuany and Gordon Koang Chuol of new development. Itang was left behind and the movement was started west ward where they came after us and initiated a fight. The fighting went on.

Their large numbers of equipment and modern weapons given to them by Ethiopian authority was an important opportunity to them. It was very hard for us to resist this fight. We were defeated up to Thiajak where Samuel Gai was killed. John Garang made thing tragic by himself. He ordered his soldiers to dugout the already dug down (buried) dead body of Samuel Gai and to give 40 lashes with whip to the dead man. This action was still remembered nowadays in Nuer community. Why Garang did this to his fellow Southerner who was also liberator like him? This action was unacceptable and it really showed that Garang hate Nuer up to the head.

The killing of known separatist Samuel Gai Tut from Nuer ethnic group by Dr. John Garang from Dinka is what has added fuel into fire. This is what was revenged by Nuer in 1991. John Garang's led SPLM/SPLA became the South Sudanese movement dominated by Dinka and opposed by Nuer ethnic group calling it as Dinka movement. Nevertheless, Nuer also participated in more numbers in SPLM/A having high profiled military commanders including General Nyuon Bany and so on.

In 1984 and some years later, senior and well educated other Nuer leaders joined SPLM/SPLA under John Garang.

Those comrades included Dr. Riek Machar and other. When Dr. Riek jointed the movement, John Garang approached him to be appointed chief logistic of the movement. But William Nyuon advised Dr. Riek to decline accepting appointment as chief logistic citing the appointment might be tribal setup that Garang wanted to kill Dr. Riek. The reason was that the position of chief logistic was entitled to fire execution when there is any cited mismanagement. He told Dr. Riek to tell Garang that I like going to front and you must be appointed division commander. As of this arrangement, Dr. Riek was appointed commander of Muor Muor division. After the movement was already structured, the communism and unified Sudan of John Garang-led objective was still opposed by many of the SPLM/A leaders.

But they were pushing together as South Sudanese seeking for internal reform and the Anyanya II faction stand as independent movement. Nevertheless, South Sudanese in fact did not left a part forever. In 1988, Daniel Koat Duoth and Dak Gai Biey from Nuer ethnic group came from western world and called the two parties to negotiate and operate under one umbrella which can freed Southerners. The Anyanya separatist-led by Gordon Koang Chuol were asked by the negotiators to compromise their demand and go up for what the Southerners were following. Gordon Koang who respected his clan men accepted the offer of an agreement and the re-unification initiative was signed between the two movements.

Gordon Koang who was also humiliated in agreement for demoting some of his comrades from united SPLM/A gave peace a chance and respected his tribe men who were also his clan men from Jikany Nuer section. So, the Southerners became united. The problem was that even if the Southerners tried to develop embryos of political ground, it was weakened by ethnic difference and sectarianism which resulted in fight among themselves.

South Sudanese splits did not only occur as of difference in opinions and strategies but also on ethnic interference. For example, The Kokora of Equatoria; the re-division of South in which bitter words were exchanged, voice raised and feeling hurt. But since South Sudanese were always convinced of common agenda which was to be free from north, no gun was bunged in tribal basis. The other war was between Anyanya and SPLM/A in which the former was called Nyagat and the later as hijacker. The agenda behind this difference was also in tribal basis. Even if SPLM/A was termed liberation [2]movement of South Sudanese, the internal rule and structure were not functioning in national basis accept it only have fighting forces. Discerned in the following citation:

Despite the progressive stand of SPLM/A, its leadership was plagued by mismanagement. In fact, the people in Kapeota and other places in Nasir (Jikany Nuer) especially Gajaak section initiated a fight against SPLA. The people who were supposed to be liberated also began to fight the movement.

---

[2]The SPLA officers gave more explanation on this part. Thomas Tut was among those officers joined SPLA in Itang, 1986. He explains all what he has faced throughout his struggle since its formation up to recent time

This meant the movement's leadership was in question. Among those who questioned the leadership style of SPLA are as follow.

- o Mandari rebellion in 1984
- o Taposa rebellion in 1986
- o Murle rebellion in 1989
- o Didinga rebellion in 1990 and
- o The total SPLA split in 1991

Those were among South Sudanese people that the SPLM/A tried to liberate from hand of Khartoum government. Why did they rebel against their own movement? One of the author's University-mates narrated what was claimed as causes that led Jikany to fight SPLA:

Anyanya II and SPLA disagreement in 1983 turned the later to exert its angry on Nuer tribe. Nyuon Bany who hailed from Nuer Fangak section, tortured the Nuer ethnic group for order from Garang saying that Nuer were the followers of Anyanya II which they called Nyagat. This split caused many massacres from period of 1984-1987, for example in Lare, Lol-gumjang, Miari, Nyawech, Liet-Nyaruaach and Tharyier-Machar etc.

In 1987, forceful recruitment was carried out. Even in Itang one, some students were taken and told to be educated abroad by the movement's leadership, instead these people were taken to war unwillingly. The forceful taking of civilians belonging was also practiced in Nuer land in 1989; for example: collection of oxen across Jikany area starting from Gajaak here to Gaguang and then to Gajiok land.

It may be good if they are taking civilians belongings while treating civilians in good way. They take them today and tomorrow come back to fight the owners. Why do movements who want to liberate its long time suffered civilians carried out such a criminal act? This is what resulted into civilians' reaction to protect and fight in self-defense when see a movement acting this way. The time which was peace time between Jikany and SPLA was time when Riek Machar came with Muor-Muor battalion. The Muor-Muor maintains peace between soldiers and civilians, and this became good time.

SPLA at a time of Sudan civil war was also accused by amnesty international for breaking international rule and convention. This violation was all about forceful recruitment which is serious human right violation, forceful taking of civilians belonging which violate personal right to property, use of child soldiers in which Jiech Al Hamer (Red Army) is an example, a violation of child right to lives with his/her family. Those all tribal setup and needs for self-determination to be movement's objective were what intensified the 1991 split.

1.1.4 The SPLM/A Split In 1991

Not only after two years did SPLM/A remains united? Gordon Koang who did not forget the unfortunate death of his leaders like Gai Tut and Abdalla Chuol united with others separatist leaders and announced a coup in Nasir, 1991. The group of separatists declared John Garang as a dictator and he is no longer their leader. They declared it that they have formed their own movement.

This decision came as the result of internal reform failure that pushes for united Sudan to be change into self-determination which was resisted by Dr. John Garang. This new movement was led by more educated and well experienced military personnel like Dr. Riek Machar, Dr. Lam Akol, Gordon Koang Chuol and others.

Dr. Riek Machar was endorsed the new movement's leader and named it as SPLM/A Nasir faction and their objective was self-determination. It means that this group brought back the idea of South Sudanese great leaders from 1955-1983. One of the SPLA officers with rank of first lieutenant narrated this part.

What results into this unrest was weakness of South Sudanese politicians because they stand against each other every moment. Since we were liberators in Sudan civil war, division was imminent exaggerated by leading politicians based on ethnicity. When we defected with Dr. Riek, Dr. Lam and Gordon Koang since 1991, it was humiliation we have seen from John Garang. That was because he led the movement as his own property as well as the Dinka movement.

We also hate his useless objective he demanded us to fight for. Again, instead for SPLM/SPLA which is South Sudanese wide movement to protect civilians, it only tortured civilians especially eastern Jikany and Equatoria on ethnic basis. Look! When we managed to resisted John Garang, a lot of split rocked up his camp in which his right-hand men followed us; he was referring to Kerbino Kuanyin Bol and William Nyuon Bany.

But after they have joined us, Kerbino Kuanyin, Nyuon Bany and Dr. Lam came up with their own mode. They tried to play unwanted mode in the movement which was what resulted into their dismissal by Dr. Riek. So, we proceeded with the new movement named it South Sudan Independent Movement/ Army (SSIM/A).

The officer also blamed his Nuer politicians saying; I don't know why Nuer are not standing together even if they see something going wrong. He was the Salva Kiir who killed innocents Nuer civilians, there also the same Nuer who are loyal to him. The Nuer politicians I appreciated in my life were those who left in Khartoum when the SPLM/A re-unification process was initiated. Those politicians were resisting coming back and serving under their enemy.

When Dr. Riek signed Khartoum Peace Agreement, he went in with a lot of politicians especially Nuer. He was trying to overcome the conflict through dialogue with Khartoum government which later resulted into 2005's CPA.

And when he decided an inclusive peace process that can include all south Sudanese, he has signed a peace agreement with Dr. John Garang and convinced him to accept self-determination for South Sudanese. At that time, most of politicians disagreed with Dr. Riek saying "we don't want to be under Garang again" citing John Garang's humiliation toward Nuer ethnic group. When we came back with Dr. Riek from north, some of our men did not come with us.

Among them was Elijah Hon Top who suddenly faced death of humiliation from Khartoum government, late General Tito Biel Chuor, Gordon Koang Chuol Kolang and others. Of course, when we see December 15, 2013 incident, it was taking into tribal line by the president. Instead, there were some Nuer who said they are loyal to that president in which some of them are now sleeping in UNMISS and hotel for fear of attack from Dinka when they try to stay at their homes.

We the comrades, who served in SPLA since its formation as a liberation movement until now, know what Salva Kiir has been fighting for. Most of us discovered it in 2004 when he defected from SPLA due to that Dr. Riek was given a post of deputy commander in chief. He was saying that "John Garang has been giving my position to Nuer because he knows that he is from great upper Nile; we the Barel- gazel Dinka are going to suffer". But Dr. Riek who still nowadays blames by Nuer community convinced John Garang.

He suggested to him that "let us give the position to Salva Kiir, this peace should not be derails due to position; let Salva Kiir come back to movement and get position". That is how Salva Kiir got the post which gave him a chance to assume the leadership after unfortunate death of John Garang. If this was not Dr. Riek Machar, CPA could not be signed and the independent of South Sudan could never have granted, instead they are against him today.

This narration really supports the claims that SPLM/A has longtime internal division based on ethnic line. This division was fueled by the SPLA's higher military command it selves. When we see this all mistakes and needs to restraint from them, SPLM/A could have to strike back from divisions which led the nation into senseless suffering.

Chapter Two

The Post Independent Period Moves

2.1 The Long-Term Strategic Planning for Building a Permanent Absolute Autocratic State

Salva Kiir for the first time came to power after the sudden death of Dr. John Garang from Ugandan presidential airplane crash. He came to power through ranks and following of SPLM/SPLA which they governed themselves in the movement during Sudanese civil war. His unexpected coming to power was a great surprise to South Sudanese both at home and abroad as well as international world. President Salva was underestimated by many politicians to carryout carefully his leadership capacity.

This was because he was a less educated guerilla fighter who only experienced militarily from his great leaders like Dr. John, Gen. Nyuon Bany and Gen. Kerbino Kuanyin. President Salva Kiir was also a head of SPLA military wing (command) since the signing of CPA in 2005. His experiences during struggle as a senior military commander and as deputy commander-in-ship in SPLM/A main stream, made him performed well in some level of politics.

Salva Kiir who managed to kept peace in autonomous state of South Sudan for eight years, seem like he cannot plan what was happened in December 15, 2013. But with great influence from his tribe men and the first most east African dictator Yuweri Museveni of Uganda, he started a plan to build a permanent absolute autocracy in South Sudan. This autocratic plan carried with it a vision of "Dinka will rule forever" and his mission is "Kiir will rule up to his death". He uses this slogan in parable way saying "SPLM will rule forever or for one hundred years.

This would mean that for those one hundred years, the chairman should be him because the move to remove Salva from party chairmanship was what caused the December 15 massacre. It means that the one hundred years of SPLM leadership plus the years' president have spent now will end after the president have already retired for an old age, and the leadership will be handover after he is away. President Salva Kiir who allied himself with Uganda president and Dinka traditional advisory board called Jieng Council of Elders were the masterminded of December 15, 2013 unrest.

The plan which was concluded by African Union inquiry commission as "it was state coordinated policy" is what caused the civil war which results into killing of around ~53,000 civilians, displacement of millions of civilians, high destruction, rapes and others war crimes. Yes! This is a plan to get rid of Nuer ethnic group or to revenue the 1991 Bor killing by Nuer.

Of course, This should be supported by the evidences in which some of these evidences should be extracted from 2013 military reform and the government reshuffling. That reform directed the entire warlord from Nuer ethnic group to go home as retirees; sacking of vice president without due process from legislature; reshuffling of ministries that led defense minister from Nuer be replaced by Dinka governors from Jonglei state and so on. As of those matters, the plan of killing was concluded as one strategy in place for autocratic state establishment.

2.2 Contribution of Jieng Council of Elder in South Sudan political turmoil

Jieng Council of Elders is a group of elders' organizations from all Dinka community in South Sudan, but dominated by Bar-el-gazel and Padang Dinka. This council of elders was formed as an agent to look for the interest of Dinka communities across the country. One of their objectives is to mediate if there is any disagreement occurs between Dinka communities. It was also formulated to present the Dinka interest in government.

It seems like GRECOR from great Equatoria and BNFA from Nuer ethnic group but differ in some objectives. The main objective which makes them different from all other elders' organization in South Sudan is because they hold the slogan stated; "Dinka will rule forever".

Jieng Council of Elders was accused by many human right organizations; media circulated news from journalist, observers, community organization and African union commission of inquiry as it was the only organization which facilitated this conflict by mobilizing Mathiang-Anyoor who later carried out the door to door search for civilians in capital Juba. They were accused of instigating the massacre by bad and tribal speeches which support the killing of innocents Nuer civilians.

This group was made up of retired politicians, retired SPLA comrades, traditional leaders and active politicians serving in the governments' day to day activities. This people have a very great influence in day to day activities of president. Revealed by a lot of independent sources;

> ''Dot-kubeny was formed as a tribal army which should give a protection on private basis to president out of known presidential guard called tigers battalion''.

Name Dot-kubeny was derived from Dinka language meaning ''rescue the president''. From whom president should be rescue? Author asked some SPLA officers whom he met in Mandeng (Nasir), they explained it like this;

> Salva Kiir and his Jieng Council of Elders planned it for a long time to fight Nuer. It was due to that they knew Nuer were going to defend themselves and they mean to rescue Salva Kiir from Nuer. If they did not prepare themselves by having extra forces out of SPLA, it could not be good for them right now.

Another officer said;

it was because they knew that Riek Machar is going to have white army and largest numbers of SPLA. This organized force called Dot-kubeny was mobilized and trained under Governor Paul Malong Awan, the then army chief of generals' staff after massacre. Paul Malong who served as politician and as an army general carried out a very great role in this conflict. He played a very successful task both when he was governor and after he became army chief of generals' staff. He was the one who mobilized this force together with Jieng Council of Elders. The good responsibility of Jieng Council of Elders is to drive a good plan on how to distance the opponent of Dinka especially Nuer who always stand bold against Dinka leadership. This group succeeded when December 15, 2013 became a completed massacre.

As all these things were derived from tribal hatred and longtime tribal driven policy, author of this book calls the elders from all great regions of South Sudan, politicians of all political parties, and communities of South Sudan;

- To be aware of uselessness of tribalism.
- To be aware of negative impact tribalism has caused
- To leave behind this tribal hatred and
- To build one love in South Sudan nations, nationalities and the people.

This call was pushed by belief that the potential of the abovementioned groups for permanent peace guarantee may bring fruitful resolution to this conflict. In fact, the conflict built between these two tribes is not new but the way to resolve it was not given a priority.

2.3 The Hand of Ugandan President Yuweri Museveni in Destabilization of South Sudan

Ugandans president "Yuweri Museveni" who created a lot of instability in east and central Africa, tried up his destabilization plan for South Sudan in hand of Salva Kiir Mayardit. Museveni was the only president who acted as a close friend as well as special advisor to President Salva Kiir for the first time in east Africa.

He is the only president who always convinced and pushed Salva Kiir to act recklessly toward his political opponent in South Sudan. Museveni was preaching his non-political toleration ideology he played in Uganda to other African countries especially central and eastern part. President Museveni who was a facilitator of 1994 genocide in Rwanda and the failing of what is now the republic of Somalia, played a very great role in south Sudan's today unrest. Museveni involves in every conflict claiming the responsibility given to him by IGAD head of states.

It is true that the security issue in the region was granted to Uganda, but this doesn't mean that the Uganda can be one of the active warring parties based on her interest. The responsibility was delegated to her to make sure that security challenges are overcome in the region.

Her role was like the same assigned tasks to other regional members who were given their responsibilities for Regional Corporation. Nevertheless, Museveni use this as an opportunity to run the region for resources mobilizations. As the result of this, he is fueling more situations by supporting one group from the conflicting parties in the region. For example;

◊ His entering in to South Sudan politics has a possible negative effect on South Sudanese.

◊ His support for an un-attempted coup in first place was what fueled the situation that led government of South Sudan to kill her own civilians for baseless claim.

◊ The dropping of cluster bomb in South Sudanese land by Museveni government was an early indication that the Uganda is not coming for peace in South Sudan.

A peace guarantor is someone who cares for dear life of innocent civilians and the resources of nations. But Uganda was later killing the South Sudanese civilians and destroying the natural resources by dropping the internationally banned chemical weapon during South Sudan civil war.

Ugandan army started coming to South Sudan as a task force for African Union to search their rebel "Joseph Konyi"in South Sudan land. They were given a base in eastern Equatoria to carry out their search operation there. In unexpected circumstance, Yuweri Museveni starts to penetrate in to South Sudan politic siding with president Salva.

It was alleged that the influence which led to the dismissal of cabinets and party's senior members was from him. The author of this book met up with remark of president Museveni displayed in SSTV during his summer visit to South Sudan on July nine (Independence Day ceremony) since 2013. Museveni shown on SSTV narrating a parable saying;

If you are a very thin man and weightless who cannot be able to fight fat man and you are holding a piece of stick in your hand. You see that fat man is coming to you, to fight you, what can you do? He asked. As a man who cannot be able to fight, you can use that stick and hit the fat man. So, you would become free.

When this was analyzed and interpreted, the author and other South Sudanese citizens who watched the channel has concluded it that this person is playing another mind game in south Sudan's political arena. Really! This parable became true when President Salva Kiir order decree of dismissing the long time served first vice president of Republic of South Sudan and de-function of all offices accept his own office.

This happened after a few days of Museveni remark. It means to author that he is Salva Kiir who was referred by Museveni as a thinnest guide because he is not well educated like his opponents. President Salva was also a less equipped politician lacking political capacity compared to his opponents. But in case, he was holding a stick because he is a president having a power to dismiss these men. So, he becomes free.

The fattest man to be hit was Dr. Riek and other opponents whom he referred as somebody who wants to fight the president for the fact that they publicly challenge the president to contest for chairmanship position. After the broke out of war in evening of 15 December, Museveni troops came to Juba in early hours of 16th December before government reinforcement outside the city.

Ugandan forces for the first time came in pretend of withdrawing their civilians living in Juba which include the diplomat (embassy workers), business person and the sex workers who rock up the Juba city. The sex workers of Ugandan national living in Juba city were more in number conducting the sexual business by money. This business was not even practiced by South Sudanese themselves.

They occupied the residential areas of Juba specially Jebel market and Customs in higher numbers. The Uganda is the leading neighboring country having a lot of citizens living in South Sudan. Nevertheless, Uganda appear shortly as something which became part of the war in South Sudan. In totality, Museveni appeared as somebody who started it early by playing a bad policy on South Sudanese and he is the one who destabilize this country. President Salva Kiir and his counterpart president Museveni waged a black war on South Sudanese in day light for unknown reason.

This was recently trace out as self-interest from Museveni and needs for establishment of long term absolute autocratic monarchy by President Salva Kiir. President Kiir who was negatively advised by Museveni has prepared for war against his opponents.

Jieng Council of Elders on other hand plays their roles on tribal basis. This was because the main opponent and the feared politician who they thought would win the loyalty of South Sudanese was Dr. Riek Machar who is a Nuer. So, this doesn't mean something better from Dinka elders to give power to this rival.

Chapter Three

The Routs to Juba Massacre of December 15, 2013

3.1 The Main Cause of The Massacre

What started December 15, 2013 massacre are the politicians' actions for ''the game of thrown''. And to make it more understand, the causes are discussed based on their characters. The autonomous state ''South Sudan'' got its independent recently in 2011 through peaceful referendum from Sudan. South Sudan which lacks political stability as of tribal driven policy from its leaders, go back to bloody civil war after two years of independence. To make thing easy and to be understand without any confusion, causes are discusses base on how the action work and how they were analyzed. The analysis from many citizens and political experts support the idea that president was trying to avoid 2015 republic general election.

3.1.1 The Abortive of 2015 South Sudan General Election

The plan to avoid 2015 South Sudan general election was seen during 2013 first call of National Liberation Council meeting. This plan was discovered late at point of disagreement when all cabinets, national legislatures, vice president and elected governors were dismissed from their respective work for unknown reasons. This process of abortion was started by president for decreeing the army reform and later developed into national politicians. These are some verification evidences on how this plan was carried out.

3.1.2 Humiliating Presidential Decrees

The decrees carried out by president were over anyone's expectation. They were only the politicians having discovered some facts regarding the actions and political move of the president. The talks of president's opponents during the year 2013 was "Salva Kiir is going toward dictatorship tendency". [3]It was discovered late that President Salva Kiir acted recklessly because he had a hidden agenda. This undisclosed agenda became the war he has declared in December 15, 2013. Nobody knows what pushed the president for the first time. But his motive was lately discovered as a move to avoid 2015 general election. The presidential decrees throughout his new strategy during 2013 were discussed in the next page.

---

[3] INSA captured the cable of military and police demobilization letter on January 2013 through air. The demotion reason which was circulated to some elites within SPLA was also discovered through this intelligence source. The SPLA army who were demoted was in documented list but was hard to get them all on fear for security issues.

I. Decree of Demobilizing Military and Police Generals

Mr. President started his move by ordering the statement stated "not confirm". This word "not confirms" was technically derived by the president and his circle. It was not known to anybody in South Sudan out of its designers. But it was on other hand discovered by international intelligence operation. This plan came out as a meant to eliminate the Nuer who dominated the SPLA. The plan was derived as of allegation that the Nuer has 70% in SPLA "the national army". To let you understand the fact that this plan was derived on tribal manner rather than army reforms, it resulted in to dismissal of around 271 Nuer officers having different ranks from different barrack of SPLA. How did he start it? Question asked by author during interview session. Revealed by one SPLA officer:

He ordered the retiring of some generals on their unwilling, removing them from national army as a mean of reform. Most of these generals were those who struggled together with him in 21 years of struggle. These are some of their profile whom everyone needs to know:

◊ Some of them were not been part of Khartoum government

◊ Most of them were those who struggled from the movement of Anyanya I, Anyanya II and then the SPLA.

◊ Most of them were among the formers members of SPLM/SPLA liberation movement

◊ They were the most powerful Generals among the other in SPLA

◊ They were the generals with more experience in SPLA than the others
◊ They were the generals with more military tactics and mostly respected by the army of SPLA per their behavior, braveness and military orders they exercise.

On Friday 21/01/2013, Salva Kiir issues a surprise decree as a mean of national army reform; a reform which was decided by him. He dismissed around 35 Generals from operating as national army "6 Lt Generals and 29 major Generals". Those generals were the most known opponent to him. Everyone was confused for the first time because he dismissed them from all great regions of South which is Upper Nile, Equatoria and Bar el ghazel. But some days later, it happened that the number which was dismissed from Nuer army officers exceeded other tribes in South Sudan.

Those dismissed generals from army were the highest ranked known generals including Obute Mamor from Equatoria, Dau Aturjong from Bar el gazel, Peter Yich Biet from upper Nile and the list go on. But for the plan to be directed to its root, the Nuer among those generals were as follow: -
1. Lt. general Peter Yich Biet
2. Lt. general Simon Gatwech Dual
3. Major general Peter Dor Manjur
4. Major General Peter Bol Kong
5. Major general James Gatduel Gatluak
6. Major general Peter Panyuan
7. Major general Samuel May Machar
8. Major general John Bol Them

9. Major general Siddam Chayot Manyang
10. Major general Thomas Nhial Khat
11. Major general Thomas Tot Bangoang
12. Major General Gabrial Gatwech Chan widely known as Tang Giny
13. Major General Peter Mabor Dhol

He dismissed them along with other officers having the same ranks of Lt Gen, Maj. Gen, and Brig. Gen descending below. The reforms order was implemented as it was decreed by president. Some of the officers' names were not published here due to lack of credibility of information for their dismissal and the sensitivity of sources hole. Mr. President tried this demobilization plan for General Peter Gatdet Yak but afraid of outcomes. He expected Peter Gatdet to reply him by sound of gun.

At that time, he imprisoned Lt. General Simon Gatwech Dual, major General Gabrial Tang Giny, major general Peter Mabor Dhol and other generals most of them from Nuer ethnic group. On other hand, Mr. President demoted and demobilized bunches of police officers from their respective work. He also promoted his own known supporters from police to military officers instead of police posts. When president and his group completed their reform within national army, they still see that the people who oppose their reform are still coming up in highest numbers especially from politicians.

Now, tensions within political elites go up to the head, where most of the politicians said "President Salva Kiir started dictatorship action".

But as president still has a power of his nations, while claimed the power given to him in South Sudan transitional constitution, no one should stop him. Instead, he came up with other decrees.

II. Decree of Dismissing the Elected Governors

President Kiir who previously accused some officials of corruptions, now wants to direct charges to the accused. In unexpected move, he ordered the removal of elected governors of unity state General Taban Deng Gai and Chol Tong Mayai from lake state whom he accused of corruption. But those accused officials denied it, saying it was because we opposed the reform the president carryout as a move to dictatorship. Taban claimed that he was fired because he opposed the proposal of Salva Kiir to relocate petroleum pipeline from Bentiu to Warrap.

The other reason was that Taban was a close ally and a relative to Dr Riek, a serious political rival of President Salva Kiir. The president's dismissal for elected posts raised a lot of questions from politicians, constitutional experts and citizens as the dismissing procedure was not carried based on constitution. As the result of this, the situation became so worst, since the president did not conduct any election which is demanded in South Sudan transitional constitution to be held after 60 days of dismissal when elected public posts fill vacant.

Within this period, the SPLM party was sharply divided and Mr. Chairman was also accused of corruption and tribalism in which he only favored his tribe men in the party, a claim which was not verified by the author.

As of that moment, president faced a very great opposition within his government especially the cabinets, parliament and from first vice president of the country. But President Salva Kiir did not try to manage the difference with his comrades in dialogue basis. Instead, he adds fuel into fire by decreeing the removal of entire cabinet, restructuring of national legislative body, de-function of entire SPLM party accept his own office and the removal of long-time served first vice president of the republic of South Sudan. When president issued these decrees, the situation was coming up more terrible than before.

III. Decrees of Dismissing the Entire Cabinet, Restructuring the Legislative Body and Decree of Dismissing the Long-time Served First Vice President of the Republic

During this stage, the tension was out of SPLM control and became the entire country problem. The entire ministers of the Republic of South Sudan were dismissed from their ministerial position. Next to this, Mr. President ordered the restructuring of national legislative body and de-function of all government offices accept his own office. In unexpected move, he replaced the position of defense minister John Kong Nyuon a Nuer with Jonglei state governor Kuol Manyang Juuk a Dinka. The motive behind this was unknown.

Within that time, some actors from Nuer ethnic group discovered the mind game played by Mr. President and tried to ask Dr. Riek to fight Dinka ethnic group. But Dr. Riek who said; what is going to spoil South Sudan should not be on his part replied "No" to his tribe men.

He convinced them not to fight Dinka as he was also supported by some communities from Dinka ethnic group. He told them that the actions committed by Salva Kiir were not supported by entire Dinka communities. He gave an example for dismissal of some Dinka comrades who were dismissed together with him from their position. Dr. Riek started going to radio station on clarification for calm regarding his dismissal. He also briefed the nation in church to remain calm saying "president have power to dissolve his government, and convinced them to wait for general election in 2015".

He told them that; 'if you like me to be your president, you have to vote me through ballot box in election". Leading cannot be fight through barrel of gun, unless people must select their leader on willing. As the communities, back to calm, more opposing ideas regarding Salva Kiir leadership system became increasing and the mother SPLM became divided which was also the root of SPLM IO. This faction called SPLM IO was composed of both the comrades who took arm and those of G14 who later became political detainees (SPLM leaders). Those dismissed comrades demanded the NLC meeting in which they called the reform, where they suggested to nations that Salva Kiir become dictators. Having this difference intensified, nation went on up to the unexpected broke out of war on December 15, 2013.

IV. The Root of SPLM/SPLA In Opposition

The author expects that this may happen to surprise all of you as you can see the root of SPLM IO being written to be appeared before conflict. SPLM party to have opposition faction within itself was said to be before December 15. What becomes SPLM/SPLA IO today is the only faction that was formed as a resistance movement after incidence. Before December 15, Dr. Riek, Pagan Amum, Rebecca Nyandeng along with other comrades were the same members of SPLM IO later divided since Dr. Riek went up for army to resist the regime of Salva Kiir through barrel of gun. And the others who later became G-10 went up for unarmed resistance movement. SPLM ruling party sharply divided itself during internal struggle for reform and arrangement related to 2015 general election. That was where SPLM IO became another faction. This logic is exposing to you the political standpoint of the comrades who were fired after the fallout within in SPLM. The fired politicians formed their own block and opposed Salva Kiir with his comrades serving in government.

They called themselves SPLM leaders while Kiir and his group on other hand were acting oppositely to them. The SPLM became a party having two blocks each opposing the other one even before the outbreak of war. This happened to be where the root of SPLM IO was extracted. President Salva Kiir who tried his best to won loyalty of some Nuer politicians, succeeded in some circumstance. He made the politicians who opposed Dr. Riek close friends to him.

Salva Kiir who was advised by both regional advisors especially Museveni, national advisors and the tribal advisory board "JCE", carry out this plan as a political campaign. The campaign stage was set to distance other Nuer politicians from Riek Machar. Mr. President and his circle uses convinced question that stated "why are you all Nuer looking for Riek Machar only to be a leader and to contest for presidential post, while you are educated, having a doctorate like him, military background, as well as you all struggle like him during South-North civil war? This question for those who have presidential ambition is more powerful.

This is because many Nuer Politicians thinks that he is Dr. Riek Machar who let them down not to reach their ambition because the ground was controlled by him. As the result of this campaign, the president succeeded in winning the loyalty of some top Nuer politicians most of them ministers, governors and military leaders. This became great achievement from president and his circle.

These achievements help the president throughout the conflict in which those Nuer politicians whom he won their loyalty contributed well. If we can see Dr. Nguen Minytuil, he contributed both military and politically because the governor has Bul militia in Bentiu, entirely commanded by his own brother Gen. Bapiny Minytuil and directly commanded by their uncle Gen. Puljaang. On other hand was Gen. James Hoth Mai who was the army chief of generals' staff when the killing was carried out by Dinka soldiers.

He didn't show any action to stop the war by military order, instead he just help the killers by convincing the approximated numbers of 40 guards of Dr. Riek Machar to surrender their weapons to the killers for their survival otherwise they maybe kill. The young men drop their guns down believing Gen. James Hoth who they see double as their leaders in military and Nuer by tribe. Unexpectedly, those guards were killed without one being survived by Dinka soldiers. General James Hoth claimed that he was acting not to be considered by Dinka as he took side because he stops this tribalism since he was in high school.

Of course, This may be the case because tribalism is what destroys the nations. If other can think like James, peace may have held in South Sudan. But as a human and a chief of army, what was expected from him was to acts as a government military general who was in command of entire army in the country and have a power to stop war. If he stopped those killers by military orders, these innocents' life shouldn't be perished; if not! He can't call those guards to surrender their weapons; if they can, they might try to defend their life. But since he hesitates to use his power waiting for president to direct him, the thousands live perished in his eye from his own tribe. Out of the above-mentioned individuals, many other politicians and army also contributed in their own meant. This was what diverted the tribal war to be political war; it was because there were politicians and army generals from the Nuer and Dinka in both sides of the warring parties.

⁴ Chapter Four

The Juba Massacre of December 15, 2013

Juba massacre was carried out in evening hours of December 15, 2013 in capital city of South Sudan "Juba". The massacre was started as a clash between presidential guard unit in garrison. But the atmosphere was full of disorder before this clash. The town was in full tension during the week of National Liberation Council meeting. This tension was caused by difference within political elites and the air was full of claim which stated that Nuer soldiers in presidential unit should be disarmed. In evening hours of December 15, war broke out in presidential guard unit as the disarmament claim. What became a bloody civil war was started as a political debate within SPLM leading political party. But it was later diverted into civilians cleansing by tribal hatred especially from the president and his circle. Of course, There were a lot of evidences which show that this unrest was triggered by president of the country.

---

⁴ This portion covers all the main stream of the study in this book. The discerned citations in this chapter were directly obtained from African union commission of inquiry report, Human Right Watch report, UNMISS report and so on. All the background and actions in the war has been discussed here. The SPLM/A actions before and during the incidence are the focus in this chapter

President Salva Kiir addressed the National Liberation Council (NLC) meeting on 14 of December with war speech while in angry mode. At the morning of December 16th, he has shown up in SSTV wearing military uniform and singing military song in Dinka language. Within that day, he was the one who ordered the curfew saying that "Riek Machar and his supporters are here in Juba; they did not go anywhere, go and hunt them down".

Who are the supporters of Riek Machar? Author asked this kind of question during finding. The answer which was given by respondents was: **"they are the Nuer"**. One of the respondents explained;

Even if there were some elements from other tribes who followed him referring to "Dr. Riek", nobody can identify them accept if they were in combat of large made up division Up to the point of killing, the secretly trained Mathiang Anyoor knew that the supporters of Riek Machar were mostly Nuer. Now, they started house to house search targeting Nuer based on their ethnicity. Within three days of targeted killing in capital Juba, 20,000 Nuer perished in hand of Mathiang Anyoor with order from president Salva Kiir Mayardit.

4.1 The Immediate Cause of War

4.1.1 Background of the National Liberation Council (NLC) Meeting in Juba

The tensions within political class exploded at the meeting of the National Liberation Council in Juba on December 14-15, 2013. The immediate background to the December meeting of the NLC was a split in the leadership of SPLM with several leading members, Vice President Dr. Riek Machar, SPLM Secretary General Pagan Amun, and Madam Rebecca Garang, the widow of the late Dr. John Garang publicly announced their intention to challenges the chairman and should run for the post of Chair of the SPLM, and thus the President of the country. President Salva Kiir removed executive powers from Dr. Riek in April 2013 for unknown reason up to July when he totally fired him from vice president. In July, he dissolved the government, removing Dr. Riek and others prominent SPLM leaders from their respective office.

This resulted into sharp split within SPLM where the opposing politicians alleged that some of the dismissing processes were carryout unlawfully. On July 25, Dr. Riek called a press conference saying the President has a right to remove me from state office. Soon after,
President Salva Kiir began a tour to entire Bahr el Ghazal region, giving public speeches that were televised on South Sudan Television. These speeches focused on his reasons for sacking Dr. Riek Machar and the reshuffling of cabinets.

This dissolvent of the government became the focus of a growing public debate as more and more voices called for an end to "hate speeches". In citation; a member of Dr. Machar's SPLM/A IO delegation, explained to the African Union Inquiry team in Addis Ababa. He explained:

Salva toured Bahr el Ghazal regions, referring to the four states; Wau in Western Bahr el Ghazal, Aweil in Northern Bahr el Ghazal, Kwajok in Warrap, Rumbek in Lake. Speaking in Dinka language "I have removed Riek" and people were saying we would. In Lake, "he said I have now decides to fight my enemies and my nick name is Tiger, I have decided to scratch anyone who opposes me".

Despite the claims by this delegate, the inquiry team commended that it was unable to get transcripts of these speeches of their television coverage. Author is not sure if the transcripts of these speeches were denied access to the commission due to sensitivity of case or if this claim is totally unrealistic. When Chairman, Salva Kiir called for the National Liberation Council to meet on December 14, many feared that the stage was set for a showdown. There were several attempts to postpone the meeting of the NLC. Discerned from the following citation; a former government senior military intelligence officer explained.

The chairman of the SPLM, Salva Kiir and his members of the Political Bureau started to have problems in 2009. I was Deputy Director of military Intelligence and tried to engage the President to get him to meet his detractors.

We told him that if there were cracks, Khartoum will exploit them and independence will be delayed. When elections came, we convinced Salva to take Riek as his deputy so there would be no problem. From 2010, no file would go from President to Vice President and none from the office of the Vice to the President. All files went directly to the Ministry. The Party too was not working. We were shuttling between the President and the Vice President, telling them of the danger of the situation but we could not succeed. Both leaders turned to a sectarian way of doing things. Nuer politicians who had sided with Salva were telling him that Riek has no support among the Nuer. I advised Salva in June that it's better to manage Riek than to remove him. He said I cannot take him anymore this one is not going to be like 1991, if Riek would do anything, he is going to face it. I told him, Then the people will also suffer, what will be the end game?

On December 5, the issue came up that the dismissed SPLM leaders wanted to organize a press conference in Juba at the mausoleum of Dr. John Garang. The President called us together and asked our opinion saying "he was going to give orders for their arrest". We dissuaded him by telling that we will all be refugees then. Wani will not be able to handle the situation in Juba and Riek is more powerful, let them go to the party headquarter. I managed to convince the Minister of Security and the Director of Internal Security in Juba; together we managed to convince the President. On the 12th of December, Salva went to the burial of Mandela and the press conference went ahead.

The Vice President did a counter press conference; "we decided to stop the NLC meeting". James Hoth the army chief of staff was in Australia, General Taban Deng Gai agreed. We managed to get the dismissed leaders to stop their rally on the 14th on condition that the President stops the NLC. But the President could not be stopped.

The officer's explanations cover the most part of background of misunderstanding between SPLM politicians since then up to the period of December 15. The internal wrangling for political reforms and lack of toleration from leading politicians were the causes for unrests of December that led to the losses of thousands lives and millions displacement of South Sudan people. Cited from the former chief of general staff remark to African Union Commission of Inquiry:

> We managed the situation when Riek was removed as Vice President, we talked to Riek. I congratulated him for dealing with the situation well. I went to see the President and told him "you can remove them but have a dialogue with them" but he refused. He even refused to talk to the ministers he had dismissed. He was depending on the Dinka ministers who feared they would be elbowed out if there was dialogue.

The leading military chief explained the situation that blames the president for negligence on the matter. It was known to those leading elites that there might be something which is going to happen.

But due to leadership failure and negligence, no single official deal well to prevent the looming problem which broke out as a massacre in December 15, 2013. Another explanation came as of remark from the Chair of the High- Level Panel, former President of South Africa Thabo Mbeki. In his remark to the Commission, he explained;

"During 2013, when differences within SPLM became public, the SPLM leadership set up a Commission headed by Deng Alor Kuol to reconcile the two factions. They kept us informed about the work they were doing. They said that if they failed in the event, they would ask our panel to intervene. Generals in the army spoke to us and said when it becomes necessary to intervene, we should be ready because if there was no reconciliation, the SPLA would split and there would be civil war. Per their report; Deng Alor reported it in May/ June that his committee had failed; he asked us to intervene which we did.

Deng Alor reported that there was going to be a convention of SPLM in 2014 during which the party would elect a Chairperson who would become the party's candidate in the 2015 general election. Four persons had expressed their interest to be candidates for the position of Chairperson of SPLM. They were Salva, Machar, Pagan and Rebecca; also, James Wani Igga had said he would run if President Salva could not. Mac Paul, the Chief of Army Intelligence was liaising with us, he warned of possible civil war. Dr. Majak Agot Deputy Defense Minister, one of detainees, said so even more forcefully.

The explanation of high level panel chairman was the result to their contact when SPLM fail internally to handle its problems. But during their intervention, the help they have exerted to handle the failure in SPLM was not disclosed while the chairman said they did it when asked to intervene. The other report cited from commission was about question asking the president on the problem in his country. He explained.

"The problem was personal ambition, everyone wants to be president. My problem was that Riek Machar was acting outside the processes of SPLM. He said it was a reflective of an old problem. Even his breakaway in 1991 was driven by similar personal problems. Rebecca was not campaigning. Pagan was lobbying, but was not as vocal as Riek".

The above question to president was also asked to opposition about the problems and how this problem was solved. Their explanation has a very great different from the president's explanation and it was like this: Salva is a good military commander, but does not have the capacity for political leadership. He should hand it over to those who can suit for it. Our press statement of December 6 spelt this out: "incompetence, deviating from party policies, creating conflict between South Sudan and neighbors". We proposed three things.

"One, the public campaign should stop, all matters in dispute need to be discussed within the party".
"Two, the Political Bureau should meet and these issues should be resolved in it".

"Three, no disciplinary action should be taken against anyone at least none, until after the meeting of the Political Bureau. This was in the last week of November. We said we would be ready to sit as observers at the Political Bureau meeting and if necessary, even intervene. We met before Dr Riek and others were removed and thereafter. In July meetings, the group with Dr. Riek spoke of their willingness to reconcile with President Salva Kiir and solve our problems quietly for a win-win solution. When we saw the new Vice President in November and asked why the Political Bureau had not met, he said the Political Bureau had met four times since March but had failed to find a way forward.

There was no point in calling a 5th meeting Instead; they would call a meeting of the higher body. He said their stated willingness to reconcile is faked; they just want to go back to their government positions, which they think is their entitlement. President Mbeki explained:

"the last time I discussed this question with Salva was the memorial meeting for Mandela in December. I asked him what would happen to others who had been removed from government positions. He said they can attend the NLC as its members. We did not expect the situation to degenerate to this point. None of the things about which they were differing were cause enough for civil war. The resort to arms took us to surprise, former president Mbeki concluded."

Church leaders from South Sudan also tried their best to catch short and handle the problems as church leaders' initiative because men of God are disciplined persons that can participate in peace building. In report compiled by African Union, one of the church leader told that he met the two leaders; President Salva Kiir and former Vice President Riek Machar several times. He further narrated an idea.

As late as the morning of December 14, I advised them to postpone the meeting but my advice was ignored. The church leader narrated on the two leaders' difference between 2010 and 2013. Both times, the SPLA leadership was deeply divided. In 2010, there was a dialogue in Yei for five days. After that the president called us to reconcile the other parties with SPLM, an initiative that gave them an opportunity to go for a referendum.

The full idea of the problems was received in the opening day of the NLC meeting. On December 14, fear was confirmed early that there may be problems that would lead to outbreak of war. Discerned from the following citation; Peter Adwok Nyaba, former Minister in the government revealed;

When Salva got up to talk, he was on a war path; attacking those who express their willingness to contest for chairmanship position. He was saying that they want to take his power. In the second day, Pagan Amum as Secretary-General of the party was told not to attend the NLC meeting, Dr. Riek too refused to attend.

In that evening, shooting occurred in presidential guard of tiger battalion under Maj. Gen Marial Chinuong. It started at the army headquarters and spread out all over town. General James Hoth Mai, the former Army Chief of General Staff concurred: the speech of the President at the opening of the NLC meeting contributed for 70% in this problem.

The meeting of the NLC took place against a rumor laden crisis atmosphere. A sense of a protracted crisis had permeated the public sphere ever since the dismissal of the cabinet and the vice president of the republic. The atmosphere was rife with rumors which talk of possible breakdown leading to a split in the army and civil war.

Both are to be blame, but president Salva kiir should be blamed more because he is president of the republic. I freed myself from this tribalism since I was in high school. We even discussed that we should arrest these people but we had a problem. The Dinka could not understand that I was trying to rescue them; they may think that I am acting as a Nuer. So, we said we do not do this, the top army General concluded.

As stated in all above interviews, the author conclude that they are the actions of politicians having a weak political ideology engulfed the young nation into today chaos. The country is weak both in army and in politics. Look! The SPLA which stand as a countrywide defense force divided itself along politicians based on ethnicity.

What if the top military commands declared an arrest to those suspected individuals who want to take this country into mess of today? The problem is because the politicians are not different from army, instead of army chief of generals' staff, president by himself is the leading commander of SPLA.

This really means that things cannot work in expected way. But at a time of risk, the army who served in direct commands needs to act on their own command to ensure law and orders for protections of the nations. The author questions the patriotism of SPLA toward their land. If this army stands for defending law of the land, those politicians starting from president himself could be controlled and the way forward might be maintained based on military rule up to the time of election. No matter who is commander in chief or the rank and file because the direct commanded generals including chief of general staff can act in mean of rescuing the country from collapse. But due to lack of their patriotic acts, they failed to do so; rather divided along ethnic line.

4.1.2 Presidential Guard Clash in the Evening of December 15, 2013

The clash between presidential guards occurred in the evening hours of December 15, 2013 as the results of disagreement between politicians. The rumors of disarmament on Nuer ethnics group in tiger battalion was the cause to the first fire of bullet. Discerned from the following cited report; Major General. Mac Paul, former Director of Military Intelligence revealed on the web of rumors that were the beginning to the root of clash:

On the 11th, a lot of rumors were going around that Salva Kiir has ordered the disarmament of Nuer in the Presidential Guard. From 10th to11th of December, Gen. Taban Deng called me saying we have heard that there is impending disarmament of the Nuer from barracks. I called Major General Marial, Commander of the Presidential Guard, he denied the rumors. We had the old regulation that all guns must be keeping in the armory. This rumor spread within certain sectors but there was no public disclaimer instead, there was a counter rumor that Salva has mobilized his own tribe in Bahr el ghazel. He stationed them in Luri near his farm. The allegation was that he has brought 7000 army from Bahr el Ghazal. This force was 311, because 10 of them died in training.

The explanation of leading chief intelligence in military was not verified by the author as there was other contradicting explanation within the government officials by themselves in which some of the estimated numbers of this force was given as 3000 and so on. There were also many others account which focused on the trigger that sparked the violence in the army headquarters on the evening of the 15th.

Within those accounts, there were at least three different explanations also acquired by African Union Commission of Inquiry. Those three accounts were like: a coup attempt by the opposition; an attempt to disarm Nuer soldiers; and an attempt by Nuer soldiers to break into the armory. Revealed by the editor of one of the two non-government dailies in Juba;

The head of the Presidential Guard tried to disarm Nuer soldiers. Major General Marial Chinuong Yol Mangok, the commander of the Presidential Guard otherwise known as the Tiger Battalion discounted this as false information, explaining that: people not on duty leave their arms in the armory; only those on duty carry arms. General James Hoth Mai concurred: We do not allow soldiers to go to sleep with their guns. There was no attempt to disarm anyone; we had two colleagues on duty that day. People were mobilized to break the armory. There was no attempt to keep a group from being on duty that night. The Commander was a Nuer; he killed his deputy, a Dinka who was refusing for the armory to be opened. That same night, people came and broke the armory.

This account was in consistency with that of the commander of the Presidential Guard. On other hand, both explanations on army generals contradicted the claim by President Kiir on December 16 that there had been a coup attempt. President Salva Kiir on 16 of December appeared in military uniform saying "Riek Machar and his colleague attempted a coup but they were defeated". Major General Marial Chinuong Yol Mangok on his account revealed:

"I reported a mutiny in my garrison. When the shooting spread beyond my garrison to town, I could not give it a name".

The Director of Military Intelligence, Major General Mac Paul shed further light on this.

"Breaking into armory was a response to rumors. Nuer mobilization started when the killing began on the 17th and 18th of the December".

Discerned from the following citation; the interviewed Editor of Juba Monitor revealed when asked: What happened on 15 December? His response was:

My office was not very far from where the President and Dr. Riek stayed. Each would bring people from his own tribe as Presidential Guard [protectors of President and Vice President]. On the 16th, the army came in and founded Dr. Riek's house which had 15 or more than 15 guards. They came with tanks, destroyed the place completely and killed all guards. They also destroyed the house of Gier Chuang Aluong, one of the former detainees. The President spoke in his fatigue on the 16th. My reporter saw three vehicles full of dead bodies from the hospital being taken somewhere. The government wants only negative reporting. A month later, I wrote that atrocities had been committed in Juba and gave this as an example. I also wrote that people of Gudele said; thousands of Nuer was killed in Gudele. I was summoned by security; my telephone was tapped for talking to Alfred Lado gore, Riek Machar's deputy.

One independent source on ground communicated to comrade in SPLM/IO clarified to author that those seen brought from hospital by editor of Juba monitor and took somewhere, were brutally and discriminately killed by one of the Dinka female minister from the government called Awut Deng Achuil. The verification was like:

> On December 15 at around 11 pm, Madam Awut Deng in a company of 35 heavily equipped body guards commanded a searches and mob operation for the wounded and sick Nuer in Juba teaching hospital. When entered in to hospital, she called only Dinka doctors and conduct little meeting with them. The background of their meeting was explained to be asking the doctors to corporate with her and to reveal where about of Nuer patient in the hospital. Two doctors accepted the request and walked into hospital with her. Within that time, she ordered her guards to kill those Nuer patients within hospital irrespective of children, women, old people and wounded innocent civilians who escaped to hospital for treatment. The other doctors who tried their best convincing the minister to forgive civilians were told that it's time for all Nuer to be kills, anyone who should step on the way would also get kill.

This allegation was neither verified by the author nor exposed through media outlet but was narrated by the survivor who was there during the incident. Other explanation was from high ranking former Inspector General of Police. His response confirms the account painted by civilians of Juba under siege in those three days, December 16 to 18, by an armed mob. The officer explained:

The army went on a rampage. Three quarters of the army stay in residential areas in Juba. When the army controls the situation, it became very difficult for the police to step in. We buried 50-60 people in one place. We have formed a committee to investigate the killings. There is a report with the IGP. Concurred by chief intelligence in military; 38 died on the side of government and 59 on the other side during the fighting in barracks on 15th, of December. On 16th, there was another shoot out. These people were defeated at 2 p.m. They lost 22 in that random shooting; seven members of a civilian family were also killed by a shell falling on their house. This was after the President's address on the 16th of December. The President's address retriggered the shooting in the barracks. I was in the office and could not hear any counter fire; I heard only random shooting for 20 minutes. The fighting within government troops was a response to a rumor that an attack was coming; I could hear all weapons even tanks.

The random shooting said by chief of intelligence in military was killing of civilians. On December 16, the war that took place was the war which the president orders as a curfew. This explanation was obtained from the survivor as further shed of light on random shooting on December 16th in capital Juba. One survivor concurred:

The random shooting which took place on 16th of December in capital Juba was not between soldiers. The armies should not be killed randomly since they were in counter combat as of fact that they hold gun on both sides.

The armies were fighting each other as the two separate forces who want to maintain and win the fight. The random shooting was carried out on Nuer civilians thus from President's remark of ordering the hunting of Nuer in Juba. They were the civilians who were randomly shot by private forces of Salva Kiir and tiger battalion under general Marial.

In some cases, this maybe the fact that the random shooting couldn't be carry out on the same forces having their guns in hand except, on civilians who hold nothing and simply running for their dear life. The explanations given by survivors are more accurate than that of the government officers because the government workers and opposition supporters may favor their party in which explanation may fall short of negligence. Most of the government officials also contributed more information to African Union Inquiry commission regarding massacre in Juba and their telling the truth result to their dismissal by the government of Republic of South Sudan.

4.1.3 Development of Presidential Guard Clash into Massacre

As a surprise move on the 15 of December 2013, war broke out between SPLA in tiger battalion under Major General Marial Chinuong. The war broke out as of rumors on disarmament of Nuer soldier in barrack. This disarmaments rumor resulted as of total disagreement between politicians. On December 16th, President Salva Kiir announced a coup attempted by his comrades who opposed him and said they were led by former vice president Dr. Riek Machar, a claim which was later denied by Dr. Riek.

President Salva Kiir on spot started ordering his army to hunt down Riek and his supporters, and to kill whoever they get there. Major general Marial in charge of tiger battalion also known presidential guard unit and other non-confirmed general in charge of Mathiang Anyoor (Dotkubeny) from Luri carried out the targeted killing. Not those generals alone, the armed civilians and others security forces also participated in killing, especially national security service. This curfew ordered by president himself was what resulted into killing of innocents Nuer civilians which were killed in the name of Riek Machar supporters.

As the massacre in Juba began with gun battle between Nuer and Dinka soldiers of tiger battalion; an ensuing brutal crackdown by government force in Juba's Nuer population was practiced. This included targeted killing of civilians both in public places and during house to house searches, mass arrest, unlawful detention and torture of civilians for 10 days was exercised.

The killing of Nuer civilians in capital Juba was the beginning of today's unrest. This tribal targeted killing was the reason that encouraged Nuer's powerful SPLA generals to defect and form opposition force. This was also what prompted thousands of Nuer white army to joint hand with opposition force and seeks for revenge. The fighting was started as an attempt to disarm Nuer soldiers within barrack in giyada "head quarter". The fight went on up to New-Site near Bilpham in midnight where the rival force battled in confusion without knowing where the enemy was.

In the morning of December 16th, President Salva Kiir came out in military uniform, singing war song and announced the fighting as a coup attempt. By the same time, he also ordered a curfew which was about hunting down the Nuer soldiers in their house. This curfew was what resulted into killing of civilians as it was ordered by the president. Within on 16th and two days later, fighting was reported in Bilpham between these two groups; the Nuer and Dinka. Armed Dinka and Nuer civilians fought each other as Nuer was fighting for self-defense mostly in Muniki, Gore and Jebel dominated by Dinka west of Juba. Discerned from the following citation:

Opposition force who based in Khor-William repeatedly threatened to attack the capital from outside. However, much of the violence that took place in town during the first week of fight in Juba which included civilians attack and looting was carried out by government soldiers. The houses of Dr. Riek Machar and others key personal including Gierchuang Aluong and Gen. John Chuol Gakah was attacked by dozers with those inside them got killed, most of them women and children.

The companies of around 25 soldiers or above these numbers, guards to Dr. Riek were disarmed for comment from chief of generals' staff James Hoth Mai Nguth. They were killed along with other civilians in the house of Dr. Riek after they had put down their guns as of directive from Chief of army James Hoth. The Dinka National security personal also involved by arresting civilians and kept them in cell without being charged for criminal act.

The unlawful detention, torture and coldblooded killing were practiced by the National security. During this period, the command falls on hand of Dinka commanders only in all part of security forces. Among those whose commands fall under them was Marial Chinuong, Paul Malong and others including unknown commanders who commanded Dotkubeny from Dinka of Bar el gazel. Paul Malong Awan who still a governor at that time was the one being seen in texture with full of soldiers from his tribe wearied military uniform in Juba. Nobody knows why this happened because Malong was a civilian who was a state governor and became soldier at the time when massacre was carried out.

Instead of army chief of general staff James Hoth, Paul Malong by himself was the one who briefed army in many occasion including Juba and Malakal before he became chief of general staff. One of the security officer from CID department narrated small story about Paul Malong when he visited and briefed army in Malakal:

> Governor Paul during his briefing in Malakal asked contradicting question that mean he is not for national issues instead for Dinka issues. He asked the armies after they sank song of moral asking "what are you looking for now" their answer was "we are looking for Nuer" while there were also Nuer fellow in the army. This is unacceptable and something that verified the Paul Malong mission as a tribal mission in another state.

The author himself was surprised when saw Paul Malong Awan in Malakal briefing SPLA likes soldiers' commanders.

The chief of general staff and all his deputies were there but the state governor came instead of military commanders to brief the soldiers for their recapturing the town. This was very surprising, even if it's good for governor to briefs the armies for defeating the enemy, it should be better for the Upper Nile state governor to briefs them because the winning was in his state. In Lologo and Khor-William residential areas where intense gun fire took place, many civilians were killed and their property damaged as well. This was Marial Chinuong in command during this incident of December 16th.

With the help of tanks used inside the city, Chinuong managed to defeat Nuer soldiers who have defected from the area of Lologo, Khor-William and Jebel market. After defeating the soldiers, he later turned into Nuer residential areas killing civilians based on their ethnicity. This was where pastor reverend Simon Nyang was killed. The war in New-site, Manga, Mangaten, Mia Sabaa and Eden was most intense where heavy gun battle was fought. Most of heavy guns were from New Site ammunitions stores.

The killing was also going on in Gudele where one of the worst massacres in police compound was reported. This was where up to 400 men were detained and killed in cold blood including relatives of the author. It was where more people were concentrated in one little room in which some dies without guns shot due to lack of air. During night, Dinka soldiers fired guns into the room with very tinny opened windows where many of the detainees were killed.

They got into the room after they fired gun inside and checked any survivor; anyone who still breathes is shot again. No place around Juba where brutal killing was not carried out. Even most of the known Nuer politicians who did not escaped together with Dr. Riek as well as to UNMISS compound were killed based on their ethnic Nuer.

The high profiled Nuer government workers mentioned by human right watch report were Gatjuet Ruai the personal sectary of former speaker in South Sudan parliament, Manasseh Magok Rundial who was killed along side with others in his house in Muniki. Sudan Tot who served as an advisor to former unity state governor general Taban Deng Gai and his friends including Manyang Tap was also killed. On 16th December, senior civil servant, Reath Thon Wakoa alongside with three other men were killed in Gudele, a close relative (cousin) of army chief of generals' staff James Hoth Mai. James Hoth who was called by wife of late Reath an Equatoria, stressed on phone that Reath have been arrested by Dinka soldiers and they are going to kill him. James Hoth by himself replied that; he was busy having a meeting in Head quarter and send two of his body guard from Equatoria who were later alleged to have got killed by Dinka Soldiers.

James Hoth only managed to rescue the capital of Reath like cars and others belonging after he was killed saying his children will be saved by these capitals. This claims by the relatives of James and the report by Human Right Watch was not dismissed by the former army chief up to now.

In Juba hotel on 16th December, Lam Chuol Thichuong, a personal secretary of former vice President Dr. Riek Machar was killed together with his brother in Mia Sabaa. Chuol Isaac was a security personnel, he was killed with many others alongside him. The President who ordered the killing heard that his men served in government were also being targeted based on their ethnicity. But he didn't even for a single minute declared an arrest and makes accountable the perpetrators for their actions.

The three consecutive days of December 16th-18th were the days in which around 20,000 Nuer civilians' loss their life on extend of curfew ordered by President Salva Kiir Mayardiit.

4.1.4 The Massacre and Killers in Juba City

The violence in Juba city targeted only one ethnic group, "the Nuer". Those who survived either fled the town by motorized transport or has ran on foot to the UNMISS compound. Some were those who managed to hide themselves out in the neighborhood and few days later, head to UN compound. Juba was settled along ethnic lines and the killings took place in Nuer residential areas, as a house to house operation. Discerned From the following citation; One of its survivors narrated the mass killing of 307 persons:

On 16 December, after the fighting in the army stopped, they came house to house to collect and kill the Nuer. I and three brothers were pulled out of the house and taken to the barracks.

They put us in a container. This container was full of detained body, eleven civilians died of suffocation in the container. There were three tiny windows but no air at all. We were so many inside the container and there was no even a single space to sit; everybody was standing the whole day until night. We heard gun shots everyday inside the container. They also push people into the container the whole day while at 10: pm in night, they started shooting through the windows that were bringing some oxygen. Then they opened the door and start shooting.

It was continuous shooting until all fall. They opened the door, lit a torch; if they saw you breathing, they would shoot. If someone starts crying, they would come back and shoot.

This happened four times. There was one boy who we advised to lie down but still he ran; got to the door; touched it; it made a sound; the gunmen fired the gun and he was killed. Two others were injured in the container, but not dead. Three managed to escape. The following day, which is on 18th, Governor of Unity State went there and got three other survivors. We know the dead numbers because there was a pastor who conduct a pray for each of the dead. Among the dead, there were three Darfurians and two from the Shilluk community.

The above killing narrated by this survivor was carried out by the security personal themselves in capital Juba.

The gratuitous degradation of one's humanity was a marked feature in many of the incidents of brutality narrated by this witness. Another resident of the camp who is also survivor of Juba killing revealed:

I have seen people being forced to eat other humans. Soldiers kill one of you and ask the other to eat the dead one. Women were raped, people were burnt. I was a student in Nairobi "Kenya". I am not a military of the Nuer who remained in Juba. I don't know the reason why I could be killed but due to my ethnicity as Nuer. I and few who survived the killing spree of December 16-18, 2014: were presumed to be dead, this is unfortunate at all.

From the discerned citation of following paragraph, the account was given by members of civil society in Juba, overwhelmingly non-Nuer after the ethnic cleansing of mid-December. It was to recount their experience of the violence on December 16 at the IGAD-held talks in Addis Ababa, recounted their experience to AUCCISS;

We have no idea who did the killing, we simply heard bullets. It happened exactly at 11oclock, at night on the 15th till morning. Early in the morning, people started running. Shooting started again in 2 to 3: am. Nobody went out because there was continuous shooting. On the 3rd day, people started coming out. From my house, we saw a tank moving towards military barracks. People in the areas saw a woman on the tank; the people in the area were coming to see the woman. When we came near it, we saw 3 people running out. We asked why the people run.

They said they were running to UNMISS. After a while, we saw more people running, all towards UNMISS. I smelt human remains in the Gudele Police Station area. The talk in town was that all the people who were brought into the police station in Gudele were killed.

Noted by commission, even those on ground with the infrastructural capacity to estimate the number of the dead have resisted giving any global estimates of how many were killed during this period. Hilde Johnson, then the former Special Representative of UN Secretary-General in South Sudan (SRSG), told the Commission:

> "We say thousands but we do not know. We are deliberately not flagging the figures in any of our reports."

The violence ethnically cleansed the city of Juba of its Nuer population. The motive of this violence was concluded by commission as country state policy motivated. The violence which originated as a schism in the governing elite of South Sudan targeted only one ethnic group "the Nuer". It was intent and effect was to divide the civilian population along ethnic lines to destroy the middle ground, thereby to polarize the society into "**us**" and "**them**." An IDP at the UNMISS compound in Juba told the story:

> "They put a knife into what bound us, turned the crisis from political to ethnic' narrator explained".

The civil population in capital Juba suffers more than what they expected since they vote for self-determination in 2011. The poor civilians who did not enjoyed their right fully in their own country were those whom you see talking poorly like this being killed by their leaders for the political debate between SPLM politicians, a ruling party of the country. Of course, this is unfortunate to still talking about death of South Sudanese since this people lose million lives in first forty-nine years of struggle during Sudanese civil war. The leaders of South Sudan need to think better and show their commitment to restore the nations for the sacks of their suffering civil population, so the reconciliations, healing, truthfulness and forgiveness should be carryout.

4.1.5 The Identity of killers and Their Formation

The identity of killers and their formation discussed here verified the perpetrators as well as the main rout of formation and the action that took place up to outbreak of war. The formation of this force that participated in ethnic cleansing since December 15 was started in 2012. Many politicians within government of South Sudan were aware of development since its beginning. But the SPLM's weakness in handling situation on round table as containment to the problem, made this to disperse like what you have all seen on 15 of the December 2013. Bodies of killers were a body of irregulars' forces recruited in two districts of Bahr el Ghazal by the former Chief of General Staff who was the Governor of Northern Bahr al Ghazal at that time. This force was formed because of Dinka council of Elder strategy to give secured ground for the president.

He started recruiting this force in 2012. Revealed by top politician in minister of defense:

> "We did not pay for them from the Ministry of Defense, though they tried to get us to pay this irregular force from our budget but we didn't. The force was 15,000 strong, and was recruited in one area".

Most of the contributors to this portion blamed the case on Jieng Council of Elder, President of the republic South Sudan, former chief of generals' staff Paul Malong and many other actors. The contributors claimed that the armies were private militia recruited from Bar el Ghazal by the above personnel. One of the evidence was the post on Facebook page posted by one of the Bar el Ghazal youth leader in 2012. The youth leader named Agel Ring Machar who later in 2015 to 2016 became a top politician of SPLM/A IO posted a photo of Mathiang-Anyoor convoy in military trucks from northern Bar el Ghazel saying:

> "these were the youth we recruited in 2012 that have prevented the country from chaos of genocide in 2013".

This post gave a clear account on recruitment area. It also supported an allegation which directed that those who participated in killing were from Bar el ghazel and were recruited by top politicians. This post sparked a lot of debate in which some SPLM/A IO supporters were saying that this man was a government agent.

Among the people who gave roughly the same explanations, numbers varied from a low of 3,000 to a high of 15,000 per AUCISS finding. The figure of 3000 to 4,000 came from Peter Nyaba, He said:

> President Salva Kiir ordered the Governor of Northern Bahr el Ghazal to recruit youth from two places. They were trained in Luri; they were not part of any security service but a private army that Salva trained using elements of the UPDF to train and arm them. They were all over Juba ostensibly to clean the town but really reconnaissance to see where the Nuer were. Immediately fighting started in Giyeda; they began killing Nuer in residential areas where they were concentrated. It was deliberately something planned.

He explained why there is no report in the press:

> The population was told never to talk about it. They were told that if they did so, they would get killed. When these 3000 to 4,000 passed out, the Chief of Staff and the Minister of Defense were not there, only the President was present.

The former minister of higher education's explanation conforms to masses' experience in Juba massacre. Cited from African Union commission report, about this private army mobilization, former Vice President Dr. Riek Machar explained when asked about it.

> There was skirmish in Higlik between our forces and Sudan in March 2012. This was when Salva started hard preparations.

I spent two weeks in Unity State. In Northern Bar el Ghazal, I witnessed the mobilization of youth in camps. When Higlik skirmish finished; I was chairing the Council of Ministers. Nhial Deng Nhial asked the question: why there is training of youth in camps of only one place in South Sudan? I said; I had no answer with both the President and Minister of Defense away. This same force was used by Salva in Juba and elsewhere during the war. There has been an impression that 70% of the army is Nuer and that after the incident of Juba all the Nuer elements defected. Both allegations are false. A justification was being created for the training of the 12,000. It transpired later that the General Chief of Staff did not know of this training, only Salva and the Governor of Northern Bar el gazel did. We did not think these problems could be resolved militarily; we did not want to take the country back to war. The president visited four states of Bahr el Ghazal.

He gave public speeches preparing the public for action. On December 9th, a general cleaning was done in Juba by Tiger Battalion called Lau cleaning. It was done to demarcate areas between Nuer and Dinka, also with others tribe in juba. This became true on morning of December 16th when Salva said: we don't want to see any '91 (meaning Nuer) walking around in Juba. On December 19th, Salva spoke to parliament and said if you love me and my government, please stop killing Nuer citizens. On 24th, he said whoever is killing Nuer now; I don't think he likes me. Though, what we wanted to avoid "happened"! We said this man is not going to listen, we must prepare a resistance, "the former vice president concluded".

From the above explanation of the former vice president; in the quotes that stated "we don't want to see any 91 walking around in Juba" and "whoever is killing Nuer now, I don't think he like me".

Does this mean that the president was revenging the 1991 split that resulted into Bor killing? From the second quote, does he mean those who killed Nuer from December 16 to 23 were those who like him, which was why he issued that statement on 24th? When the author tried to carry out assessment regarding these two questions, many people replied in criticism. President was the one who killed the nations for the revenge of 1991 and an attempt to get rid of Nuer by killing them for him to be free. Further explanations were given by some officials and military commander about recruitment of private force of president. Obtained from the African union commission inquiry report, President Salva shed further light on this:

"The recruitment was the result of a general order and he was trying to diversify the army. He gave the numbers as 6,000".

The editor of Juba Monitor concurred:
If it was a general order, ordinary people did not hear about it nor did the press.

The Minister of Internal Affairs concurred and elaborated it:

I was the Chairman of Defense and Security. They were recruited in 2012 when we fought the North, many of them volunteer especially in Bahr el Ghazal. The former Chief of General Staff, then the Governor of Bahr El Ghazal retained them, though there was no budget for them. This was never a government program but a local initiative. They were brought here to help in the fight. But they are not here now, they went to Bor.

The Commander of the Presidential Guard, Major General Marial Chanuong Yol Mangok, who was accused by many media outlet and international Human Right organization of commanding the unit which carried out the killing, gave a slightly different version of the same story:

At the time of fighting with North Sudan in 2012, there was a general call from the President and the Vice President to join the army and fight the war. All these came from Unity State. When the fighting stopped, they were taken to the training center anticipating what will happen. They were trained in Pantet in Northern Bahr El Ghazal. They were 12,000. Recruitment was announced by the Chief of Staff from three areas, though only those from Bahr el Ghazal were trained at Luri. They were 700. The President spoke to the battalion at Luri near his farm, we asked him to talk to them.

On other point of view, Paul Malong Awan, former Governor of Northern Bahr El Ghazal State and Chief of General Staff, denied that he had recruited this force. He said:

> It is a new story to me that I made recruitment as a General. No one can recruit an army apart from the national army. There will be no budget and no trainers if they are not in the army. I did not recruit them, this is not my job. "but his contribution had been seen by every citizen in the country". When people were fighting in this part of the country, there was a national call. The army was expected to make recruitment, and regional commanders were expected to do training. I do not know how many were recruited; they were recruited by the army and taken for training.

The problem was that the explanations from government officials by themselves were not the same. The president and his former vice president have different explanation about recruitment. Also, the same top officials mainly in security services have different explanation with the president, for example the explanation of chairman of Defense and Security. The council of ministers including Nhial Deng Nhial and the vice president by himself was not aware of development based on their explanation.

On other explanation from commander of Tiger battalion, he claimed that the call was general call from president and vice president and said that this army came from unity state. On other, chairman of Defense and Security revealed that this was not a government program on contrary to president and commander's explanation.

In author's analysis; this was not a general call from the government. If this was general program from the national government, the vice president and the council of ministers can have an idea on it. If the council of ministers, chair of defense and security, vice president, chief of generals' staff and other organs of the government have no idea on development, this shouldn't be called "general program to government", instead it was something unlawful owned by some officials secretly. The other explanations were from seniors united nation mission staffs in South Sudan verifying what they were aware for in the country that they were helping to go forward. The officials who were part of the UN Team in South Sudan revealed what they knew regarding formation of Mathiang Anyoor;

> Recruitment of commandos from one area is a bit tricky. When we asked about it, we were told it was transparent. The recruits were parading publicly not in clandestine. Some of our interlocutors said this was the government's way of correcting the ethnic imbalance in the Presidential Guard.

The other explanation cited from African Union Inquiry report that expressed the official view, came from high ranking major general of national security service. He explained both who was responsible for mass killing of civilians from December 16th to 18th, and why the government was unable to respond while the killing was going on:

Up to now we have not identified a single employee of National Security participated in this incident. Rogue elements took part and some people were arrested. They were taken to military intelligence. "As to why there was no government response those three days" he had explained; We met on the 18th with Chief of Staff and IGP and agreed to deploy joint security forces from the army and National Security. We spent the 16th and 17th addressing the attack on the barracks. The National Security Council he said met on the 17th; at that meeting, he gave the directive to protect civilians.

Chief of national security was accused by many United Nation Mission projects that investigated the causes and perpetrators of war. The chief was accused that he was the one who ran up the gun deal which were used in massacre. For example; the Israel machine gun which was used in massacre was claimed that, it was brought by him from Uganda. The chief's service men (National security personnel) were also accused for the criminal actions in which they were part of looters and unknown gun men in the city. Another explanation was from leading official of Human Rights Division who comments on the killing of civilians in December 16th-18th. He revealed:

We skirted around the issue in the report. We do not believe the two explanations. The anger part may be true. We do have a throwaway sentence that these things went on for a long time; there was an element of organization. It involved elements of security forces, elements of the Presidential Guard that remained under the control of individuals.

They were joined by a group of red bercts; a group of some 5,000 soldiers recruited in his own area; trained separately; pulled together by Paul Malong, former chief of army and his involved elements of National Security.

In the explanations given by survivors and government high ranking officials, the actions of the Presidential Guard were non-controllable. There was no even a single command based on national government. The commanders were those unnecessary force allied themselves with tiger battalion under Maj. Gen. Marial. Many officers tried to get in touch with them on the phone, but they didn't listen since the word of Riek's defection was spreading to Dinka soldiers. Most of the high-ranking officials held president Salva responsible for the matter. Discerned from the following citation; Dr. Peter Nyaba revealed:

When Salva went to Bahr el Ghazal in his rallies; in his own village; in August, he talked in Dinka. This was carried by SSTV. He said this cloth is yours; I am belonging to you people, are you going to accept it being taken?

In fact, the killer was an organized group that had organized itself as to '**Rescue the President"** Which mean Dot-kubeny in Dinka language. This force was the one who participated in killing Nuer civilians in Juba from 15th to 18th of December. It was even more powerful than organized forces. This was a very militarized country; concurred by high ranking officer in former defense ministry.

The fuller accounts obtained from the report of inquiry were given by leading security officers in which former Inspector General of Police, former Director of military intelligence, and former chief of general staff were among the revealers;

I came to my office when I heard of the shooting. We heard of killing in the morning. We sent police but they were overwhelmed by military or anyone claiming to be military. I was with Chief of Staff. There was no order from Chief of Staff or Commander of Operations, James Ajonga, or from Chief of Intelligence of Army.

There was no centralized command. There could be elements who could have organized in a certain way; some certain civilians calling themselves a Major-General and a group calling itself Rescue the President were in command. Those civilians Major-General was arrested by the army but escaped as part of the breakout on March 5, 2014 concluded by IGP chief.

Revealed by the Chief Intelligent of the Army:

Organized killings of civilians began in the night of 16th. Forces fighting in the barracks were defeated and a house to house search was carried out by this force. It began in a place called 107 (Mia Sabaa). Perpetrators of this came from New-Site, a military residential area. It was a combination of military, police, commandoes, national security etc. Those who carried out killing from 16th evening to the 18th came mainly from Bahr el Ghazal.

Several Major Generals led the commandos and "Major Gen. Marial in charge of tiger battalion". Secret mobilization had happened before this which we were not aware of it. It started earlier in November. Elders from Jieng met and chose mobilizers in this meeting to protect the president. The meeting was chaired by former Chief Justice, Ambrose Riing Thiik. This force was called "Rescue the President" [Dot-kubeny]. Almost 70% from Bahr el Ghazal, in their thousands was mobilized in this moment. Those who remained in Juba are now mainly from Bahr el Ghazal. The elders coordinated with the President. The financing came from office of president by himself. Riek Machar was aware of this; He was doing his own organizing. On the 16th, some of the civilians got guns, either from National Security or Presidential Guard.

I began to see civilians putting on uniform with a gun. This was a result of the mobilization the elders had done. Elders were moving from community to community. The committee of elders was 17 in number. This committee of elders moved around Bahr el Ghazal, talked to their sons in the army. They called the tank crew commanders in Bentiu who were all from Bahr el Ghazal and asked them to disarm others in the command, the intelligence chief concluded.

The above explanation on incident by the top military commanders became something that caused mistrust and blame within government structure.

Government of South Sudan doesn't want any one of her officials to give correct idea of their own out of supporting the president by claiming the dismissed coup attempt. The government and her supporters needs only those who denied the killing and those who support coup attempt claim. The fact about this was: those all above top military officers who revealed the case based on their experience and action they have seen was dismissed from their jobs. The army chief of generals' staff, director of military intelligence, police chief of general inspector and other officers were dismissed due to their explanation on the incident that killed thousands in capital Juba.

Other evidence was waning and later the dismissals of Rebecca Nyadak Paul, a former deputy minister of information when she said Nuer were killed in daylight in capital Juba. Nyadak was dismissed due to accumulation of her cases in telling truth regarding Nuer killing and her informing tactics regarding the looming government attack on Lou Nuer land. To be clear, the journalists who tried their best to publish the causes and what they have seen during the killing were either killed, arrested, tortured or summoned by military intelligence and national security.

4.1.6 The Government Failure to Make Perpetrators of the Massacre Accountable for Their Actions

Critics were claiming that the killing might not has been investigated because it was a pre-meditated plan by the president. In sources obtained from the Commission of inquiry, it reflected on two institutions that could have put a break on the violence that resulted in a mass slaughter and effective ethnic cleansing of the Nuer population in Juba. These institutions were the army and the parliament. One of the senior commander in army, "unit of presidential guard" explained;

> We were overpowered in night of the December 16th and ran to Terekeka 45 minutes from Juba by car. The Nuer soldiers in the army headquarters also ran that same evening. When Dinka were already targeting Nuer politicians and civilians, there were no Nuer soldiers in Juba, the commander concluded.

Concurred by the former Army Chief Jamese Hoth Mai:

> Back to killing of 16th to 18th, there was no attempt to counter the organized killing. The reason was that the Nuer in the Army had left. We were only left with the Dinka. There was no way of stopping an organized killing of Nuer; even many Dinka and Equatoria were killed. In the aftermath, we try to investigate the killing; we arrested some officers on 16th and 17th of December. Some escaped on March skirmishes; we took all their statements. They were 12 officers; they were going up to Colonel. We were stopped and asked not to continue with the investigation by the president.

So, we handled all papers to the National investigation team formed by president. We were stopped by a decree from Salva, concluded by former chief of generals' staffs.

One parliamentarian concurred when asked on how the parliaments act to stop killing, he said;

this committee has not tabled any issue in parliament because it was preceded by the government formation of an investigation committee. Even before the formation of the government committee, the military started arresting individual elements held responsible for the violence. Then government formed a committee led by chief Justice John Makesh. We cannot table anything until they report it. He said they had heard a military announcement in March to the effect that most of those arrested had run away. The government appointed Committee will only report in August. There has been no explanation to the public because we just came back in session and our time has been taken by the budget discussion.

But up to now, no report has been filled instead of August that the Honorable claimed since 2014. One Nuer member of the parliamentarian committee on security revealed:

There was fighting in the barracks. We saw people come in army uniform. We heard them asked neighbors where is the house of Nuer? The neighbor pointed to our house. I asked my small boy to open the gate, they killed him.

We ran out of the house and then into the neighbor's house, and then to the UNMISS compound. I have not been to my house yet since the outbreak of war. I am an honorable here. I come here to work in the day time and go to the UNMISS compound to spend the night there. Parliament for this honorable, was a seamless extension of the IDP camp at UNMISS.

Reflection on violence was confirmed by senior SPLM leaders called former detainees who had been detained on December 16th, 2014, then released. The leaders explained:

The crisis would have been contained within the party if the security institution were independent. But our background as a liberation movement means that SPLM and SPLA were two sides of the same coin. "And then added":
Parliament never played a role in resolving the crisis. What the President had done was a gross violation; it would have led to impeachment in another country.

The above citation shows that the government structure in South Sudan was not independent as well as did not conform to international standard. The entire government faculty does not work independently to fulfill accountability, even the parliament which stand for people became the president's own chest pocket. Though, there was not become, even a single way to exercise the representative and legislative works that should stand for their people. The public post became the income post to the politicians. " this is unfortunate at all".

Chapter Five

The National Defense Force (SPLA)

The SPLA with both element as politicians and defense forces is not a standing army, even if its ranking officers may be. The soldiers are mobilized for each operation and disbanded after it. In its looseness of formation, the SPLA resembles the White Army. The only difference is that the SPLA has a formal command structure and some training, which make for minimum discipline. Discerned from the following citation:

> The SPLA before crisis said to be comprises roughly 240,000 soldiers; 200,000 military and 40,000 reserves all handicapped and retired but still on the pay roster. However, many people familiar with the SPLA cautioned that its number may be taken as no more than a rough guide. For a start, the SPLA does not have a full roster of its soldiers.

The SPLA has a roster of commanders and each commander has a roster of soldiers under his command but the central command does not have access to these individual lists. In other words, the SPLA is not a single integrated formation.

The Minister of Defense, former Chief of general staff and cabinet minister explained to the Commission:

Even the Presidential Guard was not a single integrated formation. There were those who guard the President. Riek had a personal force. Paulino Matip, Deputy Commander in Chief of SPLA, had his own guards from his own area "Unity State". They too were part of the Presidential Guard" concluded by the defense minister. Body guard of Salva were mainly Dinka, those of Riek and Paulino Matip mainly Nuer. Majority of Ministers: also, had personal militias.

the Chief of General Staff, General James Hoth" summed up the situation like this:
Nothing we could do about it, we wanted mixed units but could do nothing about it".

Cabinet Minister explained:
Other prominent politicians like Lam Akol have their own army. SPLA Cobra of David Yauyau has just been brought in. There are generals who are neither with the government nor with the opposition. They are not under the control of Riek, so even if he signs a peace proposal tomorrow, they will continue fighting" he concluded.

The loose formations that comprise the SPLA have been brought together in successive phases; among the most notable of these has been the post-1991 return of troops around Riek Machar and Lam Akol.

Then, the return of troops in 2006 of innumerable Khartoum-allied militias under an umbrella organ led by General Paulino Matip, called South Sudan Defense Forces (SSDF). Per General James Hoth Mai:

> "Riek Machar went into Sudan in 1995, with his own forces. Khartoum decided to disintegrate his forces. In 2002, Riek decided to come back. The problem was he came back as leader of a faction"

SPLA are depending on the generals who own roster of their pay lists and on their ethnic leaders. Itself a loose conglomeration of village-based militias, the SSDF was said to have been comparable to the SPLA in numbers. And yet as we have seen, aggregate numbers can only be guessed at where there is no single consolidated roster. SPLA was composed of former guerrillas and different factions of militias who were fighting alongside Sudan government.

South Sudan did not build a national army before CPA. In 2003, the mother SPLA integrated four or five different factions that had been fighting them, for example that of Lam Akol. On 8 January 2006 after CPA, they integrated different forces under the command of General Paulino Matip. Every time, the SPLA integrate someone who declares in Khartoum that he has an army. They integrated them and give them a rank. Most of these militias are illiterate led by illiterate Major-Generals.

"It was like dealing with NGOs; all with their own leadership; each sponsored by a different country" leading commander claimed. The SPLA tried to demobilize them but that was difficult. It is hard to demobilize someone who has a gun. Discerned from the following citation;

Even if not intended, the outcome of the "big tent" policy was perverse. It bought short-term relief but entrenched processes that threw the wider society into crisis in the longer run. Rather than creating a disciplined formation out of the tribally recruited, mobilized and commanded forces, it further disintegrated the ballooning army from a coalition of tribally recruited militias. Confederations of militias were not only tribally recruited but whose loyalty was to those who commanded and paid them.
Rather than a single structure that is loose and decentralized, this formation should be thought of as increasingly a collection of separate armies, all drinking from the same bore hole. Their only common connection was that they drew finances and equipment from the same source which is the government of South Sudan. Some of the old timers could not come to terms with a situation where they not only had to work in the same army alongside those whom they had fought only yesterday but sometimes even work under them.

Some was even left convinced that this was not just an ethnic divide between Dinka and Nuer. The minister of defense said; this war is also a political divide between liberators and collaborators.

He revealed to African union commission of inquiry that:

"Real SPLA soldiers who fought the war left SPLA. They are all in an organization called **"Wounded Heroes"**. Most of the Nuer in the army are not original SPLA, rather they were collaborators".

But this was denied as a false allegation from Kuol Manyang as South Sudan was liberated by everyone in the country not only Dinka like what they always talk about. General Peter Gatdet Yak, General Gat-hoth Gatkuoth, General James Koang Chuol, General Gabrial Tang Giny, General Peter Gatwech Dual and many others defected generals said that:

"We are defecting due to Salva Kiir kill innocents' Nuer civilians on ethnic basis". The generals also revealed that the killing of Nuer civilians is something that cannot be tolerated on whatever the reasons might be. This was planned by Dinka to kill Nuer, even we the generals, we can also have got killed because this was something designed to kill every Nuer in South Sudan.

Other sources acquired from general in SPLA IO camp stated that;

Kuol cannot characterize Nuer as collaborators, instead they them Dinka were hijacker. Starting from Anyanya movements up to now, they are Nuer who engaged in combat with enemy. What we know is that they [Dinka] always like sitting as officers because they don't want to hear any sound of gun.

Kuol and his men were hijacker; even the today's South Sudan independent they proud of, was masterminded by Riek Machar not them. They were also the one who hijacked Anyanya II movement and killed its great leaders for the sacks of leadership only, and later accepted the self-determination they refused for the first time. What was their statesmanship in this matter? Did they liberate the whole Sudan they claimed? If they can admit the truth, this country was fought by everyone, but Kuol and his men were **"none combatant"** and were known true hijackers.

Without our help as Nuer and others South Sudanese, there couldn't be South Sudan only in Dinka name. Those who defected from SPLA during struggle and joined the Khartoum government defected due to Garang's leadership style where he only appoints the Dinka to top leadership position. We hate his mode that he could send his tribe men to school and retain other tribes for war of liberation. Kuol cannot even say this; even recently the Higlig war that challenges many South Sudanese generals especially Dinka was captured by Nuer general in eyes of everyone. They really knew, if there was any hard target from enemy, he is Nuer general that can be send.

Discerned from the following citation, Dr. Lam Akol, former chairman of SPLM-DC, an opposition party, complained;

Part of the preparation was to cherry pick generals and makes him/her a Ministers or Governors and heads of civil service a military division commander. Generals became top politicians.

Not only did military commander-in-chief become the civilian President, testifying to military control over civilian authority and a general became the Speaker of Parliament. The law says the political party should have nothing to do with the army. The speaker is a General, the governor is a Brigadier, "and then how can political arena be understood"? He concluded.

The tribalism is something being played by some top politicians, commanders, military officers and soon. The people of South Sudan fight together to bring South Sudan of their own, nevertheless this did not work the ways it was being expected. In fact, its convincing that without participation of all South Sudanese tribes, the young nation's independent might become very hard to achieve

5.1 The Defection of Most Powerful Generals and Escalation of War

The SPLA's Nuer powerful generals defected because of ethnic cleansing practiced in Juba as of 16-20 December 2013. Nuer mobilization began on the 17th and 18th of December. It took two forms, a rebellion and an uprising. The rebellion followed a mutiny by Nuer in the army led by Major General Peter Gatdet Yak, a commander of Division 8 of SPLA, who had his own problems with Juba. Following the killings in Juba, his force broke into two; the Nuer he led and the Dinka who remained loyal to the government.

During the first two days of the massacre, General Peter Gatdet Yak and General CDR James Koang Chuol Ranley alongside others respected and believed generals who were among the Nuer high ranking officers in SPLA during mid-December massacre, were blamed by Nuer public.

In the morning of 17th, many Nuer civilians were angry with Gatdet, Koang and others renowned generals from Nuer. They were saying like: yesterday morning up to now, many Nuer has been killed; Dr. Riek has disappeared; why these generals are doing nothing? Not more than 72 hours, General Peter Gatdet with his commander General Khor Chuol Giet defected and controlled Bor town. When Peter Gatdet started to defect, the armies were in their barracks, 17 kilometers away south in Malual-chat. They had a disagreement that evening in the barracks. After some hours, Peter Gatdet controlled the base having 9000 soldiers out of 13,000 from his division where 90% of this force was Nuer.

On other hand was General James Koang Chuol with General Makal Kuol who captured Bentiu town in first week of war. Some days later, it also broke out in eastern front where General Gat-hoth Gatkuoth captured Malakal. At that time, others powerful Nuer Generals were there but have no enough forces like Peter Gatdet and James Koang. General Gat-hoth Gatkuoth Hothnyang, a re-known fighter from Jikany Nuer who later became the Upper-Nile state commander and military governor, has ceased the military service since he entered to politics as a Nasir commissioner in 2004.

At the time when war broke out, he was an official in charge as head of handicap (SPLA wounded soldier organization) in Upper-Nile state without any active forces. On other hand, Lt. General Peter Yich Biet and Brigadier General Chayot Manyang were among the demoted military officers and they were sitting at their home. Nevertheless; General Gat-hoth and some element from Nuer mostly Jikany civilians and some security forces from police, wild life, fire brigade and SPLA declared their defection and managed to captured Malakal on December 24, under command of General Gat-hoth.

After three to four days, Gathoth and his force were dislodged by government soldiers backed-up by Johnson Olony. Gat-hoth and his forces retreated southward to Ulang, Luongechuk, Nasir and Maiwut for regrouping to wage a new war on government side. On the second move, Gat-hoth, Peter Yich, Duer Tut, Sidam Chayot and acting Commissioner of Nasir county Kang Goaj Deng mobilizes the Jikany Youth. On other hand were Fangak Nuer and Chie Nyabiel clan from Lou Nuer who were also in hard preparation for Malakal attack. In February 18, 2014, they launched another attack again on government soldiers in Malakal which resulted into recapturing of Malakal from commando unit in February. This war is publicly known as commando battle [koor commandok, in Nuer].

On other hand, General Gatwech Dual Hoth, late Gabriel Gatwech Chan publicly known as Tang Giny, General Mabor Dhol, General John Chuol Gakah and many others, were among the demoted generals who were simply sitting without commanding any active forces. Some of them were also under detention.

Nevertheless, generals John Chuol Gakah defected with 32 men most of them from his clan. They started their movement toward Bor town running after the force of Dr. Riek but failed to reach them along their rout. Among those defectors who defected with General Chuol, he was him only who reached Bor town and other got killed.

General Gatwech Dual, late Gabriel Tang and General Mabor Dhoal defected with some army and civilians. They based in Khor-William for around one week and later headed to Bentiu. On the 24th of December, Dr. Riek reached Bor. Before Dr. Riek can move out toward Nuer land, white army started mobilizing and advancing toward Bor to have revenge on Dinka. Three days later, the white army met with Dr. Riek in Gadiang. He briefed them and told not to attack his right hand pointing Twic East. When he delivered his speech, he said that war is not between Nuer and Dinka but with Salva Kiir and his elites. And then, the war raged on this way which was coordinated to non-formality of SPLA.

5.2 The Revenge of Nuer White Army and its Continuation into Fighting Force

The Juba ethnic cleansing of December 15, 2013 is a sad point to Nuer community in general as well as those people who have sense of humanity. Tribal targeting of Nuer ethnic group was what intensified war to be a full-scale war and marked the standing up of "**NUERS WHITE ARMY**". This organization is composed of young men, women [indirectly participated], under age of 13 years and old age of up to 50 years.

Name white army started to exist since 1989 when the Nasir war was fought between Khartoum government and SPLA during Sudanese civil war. It was for the help of Nasir youth under direct command of late General Duol Chuol Reath and over all command of late General Nyuon Bany that resulted into capturing of Nasir. Those youths were grant a name called white army. White army in the second phase was for the time of 1991 SPLM/SPLA split which marked its familiarity.

White Army: - represent the volunteer fighters who take arms against tyrant government fighting for their right. They are not national army but just a civilian youth. White army is an existed word which its full definition was for the first time discovered from Nuer tribe of South Sudan since 1991 when SPLM/SPLA divided. Lou Nuer stood up for revenge attack on Bor community of Dr. John Garang for ethnic fight that drawback to the killing of Nuer brave famous fighter General Gai Tut. The second case reoccurred in 2013 during December 15 in Juba where Nuer were killed by government private soldier of President Salva Kiir.

When all Nuer heard, what happened in Juba on Dec 15, 2013, they all wake up, took arm without any mobilization to fight against what they termed as tyrant government of Salva Kiir. The reason behind their declaration for revenge war was because their innocent civilians were killed based on their ethnicity. Those volunteer fighters who fight for the sacks of their beloved one are called white army.

Nuer white army fought without any enough facilities like military trucks, guns, food and so on. But they won some successful battles against well-equipped and well-trained soldiers of Uganda, SPLA Juba faction and two rebel factions of North Sudan. White army in case of Nuer, as it was suggested by different scholars was called due to white ash they daub on their skin as the kind of protection from wild insects. White army are known fighter in this crisis alongside armed forces of Dr. Riek Machar.

This white army in many reports of human right watch and African union commission of inquiry were documented that they committed bad violence as of revenge attack on Dinka ethnic groups. This army is guided by traditional leaders from their respective clan instead of political leaders. As the war raged on, white army became one active force among fighting forces of Dr. Machar fighting for the sacks of their beloved one massacred in capital Juba and Machar on other hand for regime change. Dr. Riek; a Nuer elder and known prominent politician in South Sudan is respected by his tribe. That is why he tried to control white army on their movement who tried to go further for committing criminal actions.

Good example drawback to that of his landing in front of angry mob of youth in Lilkuangole since 2012-2013 when Lou Nuer tried to attack Murle and planned to turn Murle land into wild forest. Dr. Riek without fear landed with his helicopter and told Lou Nuer white army to retreat toward Lou Nuer land for the sacks of peace in South Sudan.

The same is true when he talked to Lou Nuer again in Gadiang and Eastern Jikany Nuer in Gelacial; he told them not to kill women, children and old people as well as the war is not between Nuer and Dinka. The problem is that white army could hear their leader at time of briefing but go back to their actions in some occasion as when they defeated the enemy. Some of the criminal activities of white army were being pulls back by Dr. Riek's involvement on their move. So, the crimes committed by white army were concluded from many different interviews that they could not be count on Dr. Riek Machar.

In almost three regions of great Upper-Nile mostly in Malakal and Bor, and on their way along Juba road to Jameza, white army was documented by human right watch as they have committed war crime. In other reports cited from African Union commission of inquiry, concurred that:

A more spontaneous response came from county level youth fighting formations known as the White Army (the name refers to white ash from cow dung which the youth smear into their bodies). In December 2013, as word spread via cell phone communication that there was a slaughtering of Nuer civilians in Juba, youth mobilized to move to Juba and rescue their people. This was because these age groups that fight together were fresh from campaign against David Yauyau's Murle militias. They mobilized with relative ease and speed.

The White Army left a trail of pillage, carnage and destruction in the towns and villages they swept through in their march to Juba. And as towns they had captured were retaken by the government army, there was more carnage, more destruction leading to another cycle of revenge and counter-revenge by the government side. Majak D'agot, former Deputy Minister of Defense and one of the detainees, told the Commission:

> "No one recruited the White Army; it is a tribal youth militia. They have been involved in cattle raiding between Nuer and Murle and have their own structure; they were organized on a clan basis. Someone who claimed to be a prophet came up. He is supposed to have spiritual powers. Riek had no control over them. We had difficulty curbing the marauding nature of this force. They carried out three campaigns against the Murle in 2012. When they heard, their relatives were killed in Juba, they began to move to Juba with estimate numbers of 50,000 in all.

Ibrahim Wani, Director of Human Rights for the UN Mission in South Sudan, attributed the gratuitous side of the violence:

> It demonstrates a high level of anger. He remarked on how "mid-April in Bentiu became a critical turning point in Upper Nile and Jonglei. This was where the pattern of fighting henceforth gave rise to cycles of atrocity, as one group was displaced by another.

As the SPLA In Opposition forces took over the town, there were rampant killings, reflecting a deep level of animosity between two ethnic groups giving rise to greater ferocity with each sequence of fighting."

He revealed an incident during the visit of the UN High Commissioner for Human Rights and the Secretary General's Special Envoy on Genocide:

The President spent a long time talking of Machar as a nasty anti-Dinka fellow. He said that the group bent on humiliating the Dinka and cited two examples. In the first case, a pregnant woman was killed, her stomach ripped open and the baby was taken out and stabbed. In the second case in Bor, fighters raped a very old woman. The point was that it was not about sex but about telling the Dinka that we slept with your mother, he concluded.

A Lt Colonel, an operations and Training Officer of the Uganda People's Defense Forces (UPDF) shook his head as he recounted on revenge stories.

One of these was a macabre account of "someone breaking into a mortuary and shooting dead bodies because they do not belong to their own ethnic group. As marked feature of the violence was to target women, a woman representative concurred:

I was in Bentiu at that time; ten women were shot through their vagina because they refused to be raped. One was 10 months pregnant; another was raped to death.

A former leading UN mission representative in South Sudan, Hilda Johnson shed further light on this story:

> For the first time, we are seeing rape as a weapon of war within South Sudan.

The discussion on revenge violence has given rise to two debates. The first was about the responsibility for the violence. This is to understand the relationship between atrocities committed by the White Army and the leadership of the SPLA Opposition. The Director of Human Rights, meeting the African Union Commission as one of the UN Team in South Sudan, explained:

> We tracked the movement of the White Army when they got involved for the first time. They got together in Gadiang with defected soldiered where Machar had his headquarters. Our helicopter was shot while it was flying over Gadiang. Hilde Johnson called Machar to protest at this shooting and the hijacking of NGO vehicles. She specifically asked Machar: are you sure you can control the White Army? He said, yes, they will listen to me. When he understood the implications several months later, he began to back track.

Asked whether Machar did indeed control the White Army and could be held responsible for their actions? The Director of Human Rights responded:

> The White Army as traditionally existed; they have defied him and listened to another Prophet. They cared more about avenging the death of their kith and kin.

Secondly, they looked for an opportunity to loot as they had in the past (cattle, women and children).
"They loot, they leave."

A senior SPLA General expressed a similar view:

"They are not soldiers" They are people mobilized from their houses or they are hooligans [referring white army]. They are not soldiers and they cannot be commanded as soldiers. All these atrocities are committed by the White Army because there is no command. White Army is an organization of youth. When they are in action, they are led by someone from their clan or spiritual leader. They do what is agreed upon by all. This is not a commanded soldier. Each clan has its leader even they must agree first for what to be done by all.

The Director of Human Rights revealed:

The strategic objective of Machar was to bring the White Army under the command of his military forces. Two months ago, these groups were under the control of the Prophet who then said he did not want them to fight. The government chartered a plane to go and talk to him; the plane was captured by Machar force. Machar's explicit objective was to incorporate these groups into his formal structure. This objective was formulated at the conference in April 15-18 in Nasir to mobilize them and to achieve political and military ends of Machar's organization."

Head of IGAD Verification and Monitoring Group and Director of Security in the African Union, confirmed this point of view:

> "The White Army is various youth groups that are part of local security on a county basis. There is a big population of White Army in Jonglei and Upper Nile States. This force is organized and commanded on a county basis. A General who belongs to Unity is deployed by the Opposition to mobilize White Army in Unity State. If they have a plan or an operation to take over a base from government, they have an army component; they add the White Army to their force. They put the White Army under the command of the defected army. White Army is not called for a long time but only for a specific operation.

The same point of view that the leadership of SPLA In Opposition cannot be held responsible for the conduct of White Army, even when Dr. Machar opportunistically claimed that it was under his command was shared by General James Hoth Mai, former Chief of General Staff:

> White Army are civilians, they have two motives: revenge and looting. Dr. Riek was not in control. If he was in control, he can be blamed. In sum, the White Army is not an army. It is not even a collection of militias. These are not soldiers but civilians with arms. The difference is in motivation and discipline. The White Army is motivated by a deep sense of grievance, revenge and the promise of plunder. Unlike soldiers, its members lack any sense of military discipline, command or hierarchy.

The atrocities of White Army like those committed by government forces have also given rise to a second explanation. This concerns the role of culture both in giving high regard to revenge and the need for it, while in sanctioning gendered violence. The culture could not adequately account for the extreme violence whether in 1991 or in 2013, the reflection came out from IDPs at the UNMISS compound in Juba. A woman, an IDP reflected on the violence:

''During the first civil war, we fought the north with arms. That fighting was only on the frontline; it did not involve women and children. Now I am so surprised, we are killing one another while we are the same South Sudanese''.

Another IDP in the same camp concurred:

the culture of this nation is under threat. During this crisis, some of our colleagues do not speak their languages. If you speak your language especially Nuer, you could be targeted. Different communities are connected. For example, Nuer, Dinka, Shilluk, Bari cannot be differentiated. The crisis is political. They put a knife into what bound us; turned the crisis from political to ethnic.

This war is more dangerous than the war with the North. Of course, South Sudanese were tied hard by their own leader and presumed dead based on tribal mean. These IDP talked poorly for the land they fought for since Sudanese civil war and expected living in harmony as a South Sudanese. But this fails when the SPLA stormed the nations for their leadership failure.

5.3 Escalation of Massacre in Bor, Malakal, Bentiu and Other Areas in South Sudan

The violence spread rapidly from the capital city to over 30% of the country in the matter of a few days. It was intense and brutal and targeted specific groups: only Nuer in capital Juba was targeted and Dinka in the three states of Upper Nile regions, alongside inter-ethnic violence that included Nuer and Shilluk in Malakal. Not for more than two days of massacre in capital Juba, the crisis intensified to others part of the country especially the above-mentioned states inhabited by Nuer and Dinka.

From Bor, Malakal and Bentiu, Gen. Peter Gatdet Yak, Gen. Gat-hoth Gatkuoth, and CDR Gen. James Koang Chuol defected due to ethnic cleansing that was practiced in capital Juba on their tribe. When those defectors were joined by civilian youth called white army some week later, the revenge killing and looting of civilians' property was an agenda. And this revenge killing resulted into other massacres which in return were revenged by government side under president Salva.

5.3.1 The Bor Massacre

Bor town was located some 200 km north of Juba city. The Dinka's largely populated town of Bor became site of worst violence against civilians during the first month of conflict. The town changed hand many times between two warring parties from 2013 up to 2014. Fighting and targeted killing resulted into many civilians' death in which the exact numbers was not known as many were killed in cross fire and intentional targeting.

It is however clear that wide spread targeting was carried out during first two week of January by Nuer armed youth and some SPLA element of Gen. Peter Gatdet on reprisal for ethnic killing in Juba.

Former division 8 commander, Major General Peter Gatdet Yak who commanded 13,000 SPLA troops in Pan-pandiar and Malual-chat military bases in which 9000 were Nuer among them, defected and his force split along ethnic line on December 17, 2013, after two days of outbreak of war in Juba. On December 18, Gen. Peter Gatdet control town of Bor and was joined later by Dr Riek on 20 of December. On December 25 Gatdet and his forces were pushed out of town by government forces. But with help of Nuer white army youth, penetrating from Lou Nuer areas, Gen. Gatdet reclaimed the town on December 31 after fierce battle with government soldiers. During this second attack with help from white army, government force tried up little resistance but was later defeated by Gatdet's force and the armed youth. During this incidence, many civilians were killed in cross fight and through ethnic targeting as revenge to Juba killing.

This time became hard for people who did not left Bor for the first time. Gatdet held the town up to coming of Uganda defense forces that fought alongside Juba government throughout conflict while armed youth have already left the town. Some of the most serious war fought between this two warring parties were fought between Juba and Bor road during first week of January 2014 in which Jameza battle became the heaviest one among the others war in Bor. In report released by SPLA IO and circulated in social media:

> Government force attacked our force in company of eleven flank front attack with help of six UPDF war plane along Juba-Bor road in Jameza.

Nevertheless, SPLA IO reported that their force won war over government side and killed high ranking generals despite UPDF military equipment used in war. During the time of UPDF involvement, the military balance shifted. This was because Uganda defense forces used modern sophisticated weapons, fighter jets, helicopters and used internationally banned cluster bomb, later found around 16 km a way from Bor town in February by UN mine mission service. Fighting in Bor town causes mass displacement. Most of the population in town left their home either for UN base or left the town for lake state after crossing river Nile. More killing took place in Baidit and Makuach payam too.

The fighting also resulted into widespread destruction like burning and looting by the two warring forces. Now, the situation becomes worst where there is no one security organ that can control the situation.

Police, wildlife, fire brigade and others security forces were also divided along their tribes. Even in police cell, prisoners were shoots inside the cell where fierce battle was fought. The fighters, in which some were in civilians clothing and others in military uniform, carried out a serious ethnic targeting on revenge for Juba massacre. During the period of opposition together with angered Nuer white armed youth, many places were attacked even the church. On January 18, dead bodies were discovered in St. Andrew church compound. The Bor teaching hospital was also attacked by the youth where several killings took place.

During the incidence, many civilians left to UNMISS for their dear life most of them from Dinka ethnic group. But after government took control of Bor, Dinka civilians left Nuer inside UN camp and came out to their resident. During the government control, harassment on Nuer civilians took place. Many civilians mostly from Nuer were killed some of them teachers and a doctor who was shoot on his way to hospital killed on ethnic line. Aids workers were also harassed by Dinka soldiers' due to that they were Nuer.

5.3.2 The Second Bor Massacre of April 17, 2014 on Nuer IDPs

On April 17, three months after government force recapture town with help of Ugandan forces, a large group of armed youth backed by armed SPLA soldiers and others security forces including police and national security personal, storm in and attacked UNMISS compound where they killed 140 Nuer IDPs all of them civilians.

The attack which was started as a protest by Bor youth due to present of white army in the UNMISS was coordinated by politicians in Juba. The group who were fully influenced by government agent demanded withdrawal of Nuer IDPs in Bor town within 72 hours while at the same time rushed to compound and attacked it. During this attack, the deceased individuals were mostly women and children. Peace keeper claimed to have banged their bullet to the fighters and may have averted further killing. However, this claim was opposed by IDPs themselves and the Nuer community in general saying that if they responded the bullet they should have saved more lives.

Again, UNMISS report was opposed by Nuer in camp as well as SPLA IO when they reported the number of dead bodies as 53 while Nuer in camp said the number was above 53, giving the estimate as 140. This attack follows a week of harassment by government soldiers and youth protest due to Nuer in UNMISS celebrate the downfall of Bentiu town to the hand of opposition mainly Nuer.

Government information minister Michael Makuei Lueth said "Nuer in UNMISS included rebels and they are the one who provoked the attack by celebrating an opposition attack in Bentiu". Micheal Makuei was among alleged politicians who stood behind April 17 attacks, but he said this attack should be investigated. Up to now the author of this book do not see any report on the result of investigation: may be the process still under way.

5.3.3 The Malakal Incident

Upper Nile state capital Malakal changed hand several times between rival forces, starting from December 2013 up to date of writing this script. On December 24, the SPLA IO forces commanded by Major General Gat-hoth Gatkuoth Hothnyang clashed with pro-government soldiers at SPLA barracks, airport and others key installation in the town. Gen. Gat-hoth who defected and captured the town, held it for three days and government recaptured it later December 27, 2013. With reorganization by armed opposition forces from Nasir, Malakal came under siege in January 14 and the opposition took control of town. One week later, government forces retook control of town with help from Shilluk militia leader Johnson Olony, who allied to government on secure for amnesty in 2013. Nevertheless, Johnson Olony is now together with opposition force which he always fought in the past and criticizes the government as a tribal form of government accusing them of killing his deputy in cold blood.

On February 18, 2014, a good number of white army from Jikany east and some from Fangak and Akoba attacked the town again. They killed uncounted number of SPLA commando unit which is Special Forces in the country. This force was well trained and equipped with modern weapon, taught with a lot of military tactics. But it was defeated and dislodged by civilians' youth within 45 minute of serious guns' fire.

During this attack, many civilians were killed both on crossfire and house to house search by this white army. Those who suffered in this attack were Shilluk who were the dominance in the city as well as their home land. White army killed Shilluk because Gen. Johnson Olony was with government forces. Throughout this all attacks, forces on both sides conducted house to house searches, arbitrary arrest, and killed many civilians based on ethnicity. A brutal opposition attack in February included, killing insides churches and Malakal teaching hospital. Many others killing based on ethnic line took place on their way to Malakal especially the Dinka County between Ulang and Malakal like Baliet and other villages. Others killing took place during crossfire inside the town.

The Nuer white army; wearing colored red headband, who fought in eastern front of Upper Nile under Maj. Gen Gat-hoth, fight the same cause in Juba, in which their beloved one was ethnically targeted. They indiscriminately killed those who are not Nuer. At that time, more of the population went for hideout in UN base. Nevertheless, they were not only white army who carried out this kind of activities. Government forces tortured Nuer civilians at a time of their occupation.

Those tortures included sexual violence, ethnic killing, kidnapping and others criminal actions practiced during their presence in town. A Nuer Presbyterian church pastor was also killed during the government occupation. Not only those who were priests or civilians being targeted, even those who were UN workers were also targeted on their ethnicity.

Good example was killing of a UN worker called Yien Gai and his friends by government soldiers being pulled out from UN vehicle in Maban County of Upper Nile. Other was kidnapping of John Mark Diang by government force in Malakal airport and others uncounted killing based on ethnic line. Things became worth when the unconstitutional 28 states were decreed by president in which Latjor, Eastern Nile and Western Nile were curved away from former Upper Nile state. The ancestral historical land of Shilluk was annexed to Eastern Nile of Padang community. On the date of decree, the sons and daughter of Shilluk community both in government and in opposition declared their position to fight back for their land by any meant possible.

On other hand, the Nuer opposed the creation of 28 states, thought the tension in Upper Nile get to the head. The so called Eastern Nile governor of created 28 states; Chol Thon Balook backed an incident which was like what happened in Bor in 2014 on IDPs. This was to push out from town the Shilluk and Nuer who were there and to stop them opposing 28 states. On February 17-18, 2016, the Eastern Nile youth mobilized by governor and backed by SPLA in Malakal, carried out a brutal killing on IDPs. It's unfortunate for president to circle himself and appoint anti-peace element like these men who their intension is to kill civilians on ethnic basis. The February killing in Malakal UN base was investigated by UN experts and it was clear and verified that the Eastern Nile governor and the SPLA in Malakal were perpetrators.

5.3.4 The Massacre in Bentiu

The largely inhabited Nuer town of Bentiu; the city of Unity State in northern part of the country has changed hand many times. Before the total defection of Gen James Koang, several skirmishes took place in which Nuer actors ethnically targeted the Dinka civilians on reprisal to Juba massacre. Those skirmishes took place in Lele Village of Pariang County and Tharjiath oil well. Laborer from Nuer turned to Dinka officers, killed at least six bodies using batons and machetes. That was the same as what happened in Bor and later in Malakal where security organ split along ethnic line.

Nevertheless; Gen. James Koang by himself help on rescuing civilians' life to UNMISS but at a time of his defection, he was not in full control of the town, so the killing was going on in some part of the town. Military offensives in the town by both rival forces have been accompanied by targeting of civilians based on their ethnicity. On December 21, the Nuer Major General CDR James Koang Chuol Ranley, commander of SPLA's division 4 based in Rubkotni next to Bentiu town, declared his defection and announced that he assumes the position as the military governor of unity state.

Gen. James Koang who by himself sees the killing in Juba came from the capital Juba some days before declaring his defection. He came from Juba where he was told to handle the situation in unity state. But as he personally seen what had been taking place in Juba, he plans to give the solution by only defecting from government and to oust Salva Kiir by force.

The defection of Gen. James Koang was followed by series of skirmishes between Nuer and Dinka soldiers in the different barracks of division four in unity state which included the Rubkotni skirmishes of December 19, 2013. Government force backed up by north Sudan rebel fighter, Justice and Equality Movement (JEM) regained the control of town on January 10, 2014. Fighters from north Sudan's rebel movement "JEM" have been stationed in Bentiu since 2012 when Gen. Taban Deng Gai still the governor of oil rich unity state. At a time of government advance, JEM was advised to take part in attack and promised for fund and support against Sudan government. With help of JEM, government force recaptured the town and JEM were given a base in Bentiu town and Rubkotni where they carried out several attacks on civilians in Guit and other place in southern part of the state.

The attacks by government force on southern part of the state registered the massive and more violence in which burning, raping, killing of little children and looting of civilians' property was carryout indiscriminately, mostly on Leer, Koch and even in Guit. During entry of government soldier in unity state, wide spread scale damage took place including extensive burning in Bentiu and Rubkotni. Most civilians fled their homes for UN base and those who remained at their home were targeted. During this period, the entirely Rubkotni market was burned to ashes. The government force and their allied fighter from JEM set ablaze many huts and burned civilians inside it.

The angry mob used to sing in Dinka language carried out many violence on civilians in unity state. Collected by UN personal, around 30 dead bodies were discovered along the road between centers of the town and UNMISS base. This mass killing took place as Gen. Koang's force left the town a head of government and his allied advance, after burning the head quarter of military store and ammunition in Rubkotni. Government force accused them of setting on fire the oil installation, an accusation they refuted.

Government force moved both east and south ward of the state, a place controlled by opposition force. Following the week of intense fight, government force conducts several operations east ward and later south where they have killed a huge number of civilians, burning the villages and other serious violence. The other fighters who committed this violence together with Dinka actors in unity state were Nuer sons who fight for the support of Joseph Nguen Minytuil.

These are Lt. Gen. Bapiny Minytuil, the elder brother of the unity state governors Nguen Minytuil and their uncle Major Gen. Puljang who commanded the Bul militia in Bentiu. [5]Opposition force with both Koang and Peter Gatdet in command managed to recapture the town in April 15, 2014 where Gen. Puljaang and his nephew Nguen Minytuel reported escape narrowly.

---

[5] Gatwech Gai Makuach is a SPLA Brig. Gen who defected in Wau on protest for Mapel killing. He was the one who communicated more information to many media outlet. John Wiyual Muon, 28; a mechanic division SPLA member trained in Mapel describe the situation as something he didn't see in his life. He said the Mapel killing was coordinated in advance by top officers. The numbers of trainees killed in Mapel was not known up to now. SPLA Mechanic division trained in Wau were members of SPLA soldiers but nobody knows why this was planned by top officers.

This was where many high ranking military leaders and county commissioner was reported held as a POWs (prisoners of war) by opposition force. During this attack, opposition force was accused of killing many civilians in mosque, hospital and other areas on ethnic motivated killing some of them reported as Darfur civilians. But general Koang in an interview, some days later denied the accusation saying; those who were killed were those involved in combat with us not civilians. During opposition advance in April, civilians were denied access to UNMISS camp by governor Nguen saying SPLA is in control of the situation. Nevertheless, opposition fighters who were equipped with modern military hardware rapidly penetrated with use of modern weapon and only faced little resistance from government force. This incident caused a lot of death while governor by himself escaped narrowly.

Opposition force claims that those who were in mosque were fighters from JEM and the Dinka among them were government soldiers who hided there, hopping that they may not be attacked by their enemy while in mosque. In May 2014 operation, Bentiu was recaptured by government force when Paul Malong Awan became chief of generals' staff, the violence still increasing where more killing was carryout by Puljaang in southern part of Bentiu.

5.3.5 The Mapel Massacre of Nuer Mechanic Division Trainees

Maple; located in eastern part of the state in western Bar el ghazal is the one of the largest SPLA bases in South Sudan. It also served as a training center for new recruits. The coordinated killing was started on Friday of April 26, 2014, a week after Bor attacks on IDPs. The Nuer Brig. Gen named Gatwech Gach Makuach who has defected spoke to Sudan tribune at that time saying;

> Nuer trainees were deliberately massacred in Mapel. The government said that it was an internal mutiny; this is not true, they are certain Brigadier Generals ''Baak Dinka'' led trainees who mobilized their people against Nuer trainees. He said the incident started after attackers' beats todeath an unarmed Nuer trainee in the market place and they went to camp shouting and started shooting indiscriminately at Nuer.

But other sources within government side revealed that the violence was sparked off by angry Dinka widows of slain SPLA troops. The exact numbers of perished individuals are not known as government agent including Philip Aguer the government's former military spokesperson and Governor Rizik Zachariah estimated the death toll as three or four. Other sources including defected Brig. Gen Gatwech said 192, military medical source said 150, while former SPLA IO spokesperson, Brig. Gen Lul Ruai Kong put the number to 220. So, there was no exact number on the death toll.

Furthers account was concurred by one of the SPLA soldier (a trainees) who was in Mapel during the incident. A survivor of Mapel incident in SPLA's mechanic division who was trainee at that time narrated the story. He lost his one tooth during the incident saying;

> Mapel killing was coordinated massacre. Even when we were in the camp, we monitor the work of our Dinka friends. We discovered that something will happen. But as we have no power either to defect or protect in self-defend, we kept quite waiting for the day. Speaking to him in Nasir (Mandeng); he shows author his one tooth missing saying; I lost this tooth when I jumped to Dinka soldier who tried to shoot me. I managed to take his gun from him by force and went on for fight of self-defense.
>
> We didn't know why they plan to do this, while in our code of conduct in mechanic division, we were taught that we are going to fight only for external aggression. We were taught not to even involve in an internal problem regarding whatever the case might be. But as this was really taken into tribal politic, that was why they do it like that. I know the players who planned this attack on us. They were government actors and told their Dinka generals to carry out the task. Those who were together with us afraid because we were together with them in Blue Nile when we fought Khartoum government for more than half year. They know how fighter we are in our division.

We didn't have any guns with us when we were in training camp. The guns we tried to protect ourselves were from them. We get them by forces during the incident and other from defectors who came from Wau town who join us later when we were in bush.

At that time, soldiers, university students and civilians were denied an access to UN base for the first time but later readmitted and hide out there for their dear life. In Wau, the state capital of western Bar el ghazel, many Nuer soldiers having different ranks defected, in which Brig. Gen. Gatwech Makuach was one among them. Those soldiers were angry for the killing of innocents' trainees but some of them returned when town back into calm. Wau, a town in Western Bar el Ghazal inhabited by minorities and Dinka themselves, experiences calm for two years after the Mapel incident.

But after the unilateral decree by president Salva of 28 states; the state faces unlawful action most of them committed by SPLA. In unexpected move on Friday evening and in early hours of Saturday June 24, 2016, war broke out between SPLA and unknown armed force alleged to be SPLM IO, an allegation later refuted by SPLA IO. The move came as a week of tension rocked Wau town after sporadic fight in Raja between government force and the same unknown force. In a week before war broke out in Wau, eight different cases of killing were reported and other kidnapping cases including kidnapping of camera man of Rizik Zachariah, a Wau former governor and the Raja governor of 28 states was also reported.

As of the above insecurities report in the week before outbreak of war, former governor Gen. Elias Waya fallout with SPLA division commander in Wau and sector commander Gen. Jok Riak. The governor was accusing the commanding officers of corrupting with soldier's money which lead the soldier to go and loots civilians belonging. This disagreement resulted to the state of emergency declaration by army. This state of emergency order was executed without state authority knowledge due to security situation in state. On Friday evening, the war broke out and resumed on Saturday morning. As the war broke out, President Salva Kiir issued presidential decree dismissing Governor Gen. Elias; orders his arrest and replaced him with Andrea Mayar.

The fighting caused a lot of displacement and lives in which the estimate numbers on death was said to be 400, an opposition figure of Democratic Salvation Front Party UDSF in state confirmed. Per the statement by UN and Red Cross, at least an approximate number of 100,000 civilians seek protection in UN and Red Cross compound while some of them fled to bush and other 35,000 were reported fled to SPLA IO controlled area. Resident of Wau town said that the bodies of people killed in clash stranded in residential areas of Kalbari, Kalkalu, Hai Kosti and Jebel Khair inside town. The situation was very terrible in which the SPLA was accused of targeting minority in Wau. The targeting of civilians in ethnic basis like what happened in Juba derives many citizens in the country to point their angry on president of the country. The angry civilians included church leaders, opposition parties, community based organization and so on.

One of the church leaders who criticize government of South Sudan categorizes its leaders as evil and criminals. It's unfortunate when we still hear many massacres still happening in South Sudan while the peace agreement was signed in August 2015. Why the government of South Sudan is always accused of targeting its civilians? This mean failure on giving assurance for civilian protection since the credit of this government is killing its own people. The government needs to re-correct its way of handling situations in the country and to carry out the reconciliation between SPLA and the civil population as well as between citizens by themselves.

⁶ **Chapter Six**

The Aftermaths of the Massacre

The diverted political conflict which results into civil war causes many more life and the destruction. The conflict draws many more pages where the world and the region are trying their best to pull back the civilians suffering. But the full granting of peace to south Sudanese seem to be being draw back by regional interest. The aftermaths of this civil war are as follow.

6.1 Death of More Than Twenty Thousand and Displacement of Tens of Thousands as Refugees

Within three days of ethnic cleansing in capital Juba, the estimated number of 20,000 civilians was reported being killed by government soldiers. After two to three days of killing in Juba, the war broke out in three states of great Upper Nile along ethnic line where unknown number was killed from both sides.

---

⁶ The consequences of this senseless war are terrible. Thousands were starved into death for lack of foods not even killed by bullet. Thousands of civilians lose their dear life in ethnic line on hand of two warring parties, while the government of South Sudan failed to protect life of its civil population and is the only actor who participated more than anything in civilians' torture. Millions of civilians were displaced both internally and across regional border; the properties of civilians were looted by both sides in which white army lead the upper role in looting. The national army (SPLA) became the true enemy of South Sudan civilians "even Dinka by themselves". The international community and IGAD peace process have said to disperse the looming revenge from Nuer white army.

When the war was continuing and the strategic towns became war field, civilians moved to neighboring African countries where they were served as refugee. This was what resulted into IGAD's plan to mediate peace talk for South Sudan. Not only that the war was between Nuer and Dinka, the other tribes were also targeted; especially Shilluk by Nuer white army when Johnson Olony still allied himself with regime in Juba. Equatoria were also being targeted by government forces when Juba government learned that they support the reforms masterminded by armed opposition. After one year, Juba government turned its back to Shilluk ethnic group. In fact, they were the Shilluk militia who helped the government dislodged Nuer white army from Malakal. The Shilluk militia's support for the government side was what resulted into recapturing of Nasir town from opposition.

The government's turning strategy against Shilluk was masterminded by top politicians and elders from Padang Jieng clan. This was due to their long-time conflict on land issues with Shilluk community. Their plan of turning against Shilluk ethnic group was what resulted into coldblooded killing of Johnson Olony's deputy [a major general from Shilluk ethnic group]. This was what provoked the switching of side by General Johnson Olony to SPLM/A IO on protest of his deputy killing, while they fully supported the government and fight the war on its side. The civilians targeting has been what fueling the conflict because both warring parties are fighting in retaliation for other side's action. The massacre in Juba carried out on Nuer was what provoked Nuer in the three states of great Upper-Nile to look for revenge.

The IGAD led peace process funded by international community, have says to have diverted the looming revenge killing. This was due to their urgent call for peace and the direct involvement of international community for relief service.

6.2 The Involvement of International Community

Another move was the involvement of international community. Quickly after the displacement of the thousands by war, the international community, UN and Troika termed as IGAD friends drawn fund for the support of displaced civilians. The above-mentioned parties also mobilize the billion dollars for peace talk between South Sudanese warring parties. This was after the IGAD head of states willingness to mediate the two armed parties.

The three above mentioned donors also pushed the Juba government to free the SPLM leaders they have falsely imprisoned in the name of dismissed coup attempt. This was when the SPLM/SPLA IO set the releasing of political imprisoned SPLM leaders as precondition. In a peace process, it was also the IGAD-plus peace initiative with help from those three international donors that helped drawn the final CPA II signed in August and September respectively by warring parties. Even if the IGAD peace process ended up in another war, this was up to South Sudanese for their failure to implement the signed document.

6.3 The IGAD Peace Process in Addis Ababa

It was only after two weeks since the outbreak of war in capital Juba on December 15, 2013 when the IGAD head of state peace process was started in Addis Ababa in January 2014. In a very surprised move, Dr. Riek Machar accepted negotiating with President Salva Kiir to give a peaceful solution to the conflict on round table dialogue with help of IGAD states. SPLA IO leader, Dr. Riek Machar was blamed in some occasion by his supporters who were only looking for military solution due to angry on reflections of what was happened in Juba. But he did not hesitate to appoint a representative who would acts on behave of him during peace process in Addis Ababa.

Dr. Riek appointed Rebecca Nyandeng Garang to represent his movement as chief negotiator. But Rebecca turned down an appointment from Dr. Riek for that she doesn't support the already used army to resist the regime in Juba. For that case, she did not agree on appointment to represent the SPLM/A IO. Other conflicting sources on her turn down for an appointment was said to be; she doesn't want to let Dr. Riek his boss because she was contester by herself. Her unwillingness to represent the movement as chief negotiator led to Dr. Riek's appointment of General Taban Deng Gai as a chief negotiator of SPLM/A IO. After this, the negotiation was kicked off on January 23, 2014.

[7]6.4 IGAD and the Region

IGAD is an organization formed by east African country since 1986 and later joined by Eritrea after gaining its independent in 1993 and admitted South Sudan to membership since 2011 after it gain its independent. In January 1986, assembly of heads of states and government signed an agreement which officially launched the inter-governmental authority on drought and development (IGADD) to function as a body for development and drought control in east Africa, a part of sub-Saharan affected by drought in Africa. The inter-governmental on authority in development (IGAD) in eastern Africa was created in 1996 to supersede the intergovernmental authority on drought and development which was founded in 1986.

IGAD came to existence because of a declaration to revitalize IGADD and expand corporation among member states in April 1995 in Addis Ababa at the assembly of head of states and government. On March 21, 1996 in Nairobi, the assembly of head of states and government signed a letter of instrument to amend the IGADD charter/agreement establishing the revitalized IGAD within the new name that still stand to today name [The Inter-Governmental Authority on Development].

---

[7] IGAD head of states' role was suggested by many writer and international human right organization including amnesty international. IGAD tirelessly contributed too much in East Africa, specifically the horn regions of Eastern Africa. Maboub Maalim, an IGAD general secretary summarize the IGAD role in Horn and other writer shed further light on IGAD role within region and across its border in form of international cooperation.

The revitalized IGAD, with expanded areas of Regional Corporation and a new organizational structure was launched by the IGAD assembly of head of states and government on 25 November 1996 in Djibouti (the republic of Djibouti) The objective of IGAD heads of states are to:

- o Promote joint development strategies and gradually harmonize macro-economic policies and program in social, technological and scientific field.
- o Harmonize policies regarding trade, customs, transport, communication, agriculture and natural resources while on other hand promote free movement of goods, services and people within the region.
- o Create an enabling environment for foreign, cross border and domestic trade and investment.
- o Initiate and promote programs to achieve regional food security, encourage and assist effort of member states to collectively combat drought and other natural and manmade disaster
- o Develop and improve a coordinated and complementary infra-structure in the areas of transport, telecommunications and energy in the region
- o Promote peace and stability in the region and create mechanism for prevention, management and resolution of inter-states and intra-states conflict through dialogue
- o Mobilizes resources for the implementation of emergency, short term, medium term and long-term programs within framework of regional corporation

o Promote and realize the objectives of the common market for eastern and southern Africa (COMESA) and African economic community.
o Facilitate, promote and strengthens cooperation in research development and application in science and technology.

The Number of strength that has evolved over the years is that IGAD has become proficient at being able to convene at very short notice. In 2011 the institution held 12 heads-of state meetings, and 28 executive council meetings. IGAD policy decisions are reached by consensus. Many of the issues that are discussed in IGAD are sensitive, relating to the sovereignty of member states or the bilateral and multilateral relationships within the institution. Reaching decisions through consensus reduces the risk of any possible disappointment involved in a win-or-lose voting system. There are strong regional similarities throughout the IGAD region that make it easier to conduct business and sustain links between member states.

Many ethnic groups cut across country borders. These ties enhance regional stability and the harmonization of IGAD policies. IGAD's approach to peace and security issues is unique, due to the nature of dealing with complex issues daily. The institution has developed a peace and security role that works on a local basis at the ground level. There are several specific areas in which IGAD plays an important role in contributing to stability in the Horn of Africa.

Capabilities range from mediation to conflict-prevention and capacity-building between member states. IGAD has played a mediation role in many regional developments. It was heavily involved in the Sudan peace process that culminated in the Comprehensive Peace Agreement (CPA). In the run-up to South Sudan's independence, IGAD facilitated talks that eventually helped deliver the South Sudanese referendum. IGAD has held a long-standing role in the re-establishment of sovereign government in Somalia. After 13 failed attempts to get Somalia back on track, the 14th attempt headed by IGAD installed the transitional government of President Abdullah Yusuf, and has been involved in the process of governance in Somalia ever since.

One significant capability of IGAD is its work in Conflict Prevention Management and Resolution (CPMR) through the Conflict Early Warning and Response Mechanism (CEWARN). Conflict Early Warning and Response Mechanism is an IGAD institution dedicated for securing peace and stability in the region by influencing policy through a Conflict Prevention Management and Resolution approach, producing and providing information to policy makers. This is differentiated from IGAD's mediation role, as Conflict Early Warning and Response Mechanism's Conflict Prevention Management and Resolution mechanism investigates peace and security at a lower level in member states as opposed to higher level multi-country negotiations. Military intervention when needed is arranged by IGAD through consensus and is to be deployed internally in the region, with the aim to reduce reliance on foreign intervention.

IGAD forces intervened during the 2006 Islamic Courts insurgency in Somalia and the IGAD Peace and Support Mission in Somalia (IGASOM) was the precursor to the African Union Mission in Somalia (AMISOM). IGAD member states are the chief contributors to IGAD security forces. IGAD holds a role investigating emerging crimes. It approaches issues including money laundering, terrorism, cyber-crime, organized crime and piracy on a case-by-case basis. IGAD is concerned with tackling the inland component of piracy as well as the maritime component. The work IGAD does in emerging crimes, contributes to regional and international stability. Capacity-building in the Horn of Africa is a priority for IGAD. It works to facilitate multi-country approaches to regional concerns, particularly in cross border issues such as trans-national ethnic groups.

IGAD encourages the harmonization of policies across countries, which contributes to stability building throughout the region. Its capacity-building functions include a focus on migration, trade harmonization and the movement of goods and people. IGAD works on many programs, many of which are designed to enhance regional integration. This includes but is not limited to developing and regulating a free trade area in the region. IGAD's regional integration agenda is enshrined in the Minimum Integration Plan which is based on the fundamentals member states must adhere to as
part of their membership. This is also an important contributing factor regarding security issues. Controlling drought in the Horn region is another focus for IGAD.

IGAD heads of state and the East African Community recently made a political commitment that drought must never turn into famine in the Horn of Africa again, following the 2011 East Africa drought. IGAD has formulated the Drought Resilience Initiative to operationalize policies aimed to support people between droughts. IGAD is involved in infrastructure development across the region: building roads, improving energy inter-connectivity and trade links. IGAD facilitated the provision of electricity from Ethiopia to Djibouti, reducing Djibouti's dependence on generators. Responsibility for regional IGAD programs is delegated to individual member states. The Executive Council assigns the lead role of various programs to member states: infrastructure projects are led by Ethiopia, drought resilience and resources management is led by Kenya, Uganda leads on peace and security issues, Djibouti leads on maritime security and Sudan leads the trade homogenization agenda.

Civil servants from member states are seconded to IGAD, and work for a period receiving their usual salaries alongside allowances depending on the city they are seconded to. Employing civil servants from IGAD member states an assigning key roles to different countries is important to install a sense of ownership of IGAD, which translates into the security and diplomatic well-being of the IGAD region. IGAD holds a political role as well as a stabilization role. IGAD encourages its member states to live per their constitutional rules, to adhere to the process of democratization and to maintain acceptable levels of governance.

IGAD is involved with NGOs and civil society in the region, and works on issues of good governance, parliamentary systems and female representation in politics, heading the IGAD Women Parliamentary Conference in 2009. IGAD also held a conference on federalism in Ethiopia, and works to expand dialogue on how federalism can benefit the region by allowing people to become more involved in local affairs, and how government resources can be mobilized to enhance development in this area. IGAD head of states contributed tirelessly on its inter and intra-states conflict among its members' states. The following inter-states conflicts were mediated and gave a solution by the IGAD

- o Brief armed conflict between Ethiopia and Somalia due to Ethiopia's control for Somalia inhabited territory which led to full scale war in 1977-1978 and the Ethiopia's direct military intervention in Somalia since 2006-2008.
- o Serious tension between Kenya and Somalia in 1960 for control of Kenya's northern frontier district
- o High tension between Sudan and Eritrea in 1994-1998 due to Islamists threats
- o Tension between Sudan and Ethiopia in 1995-1998 for Sudanese alleged links to Hosni Mubarak assassination attempt in Addis Ababa capital
- o Ethiopia-Eritrea full scale war in 1998-2000 for territorial dispute
- o Eritrea-Djibouti brief confrontation due to territorial dispute in 2008-2009

o Kenya-Uganda tension on territorial dispute over magingo island in 2009.

o The Sudanese wars of 1983-2005 where IGAD help mediated the comprehensive peace agreement which led to birth of new South Sudan.

This is true by looking all the above effort, IGAD head of states contribute more than anything in its member states especially Horn of Africa.

[8] 6.5 IGAD and South Sudan

In the African union commission of inquiry report, further contribution in both Sudanese civil war and recent south Sudanese conflict by IGAD head of state were cited. Before the independence of South Sudan in 2011, the Intergovernmental Authority for Development (IGAD) comprised six countries: Kenya, Uganda, Tanzania, Ethiopia, Djibouti and Sudan. IGAD's involvement in the civil war in Sudan gathered steam after the formation of a group of three countries; the USA, the UK and Norway then called "Friends of IGAD," and more recently the Troika. Hilda Johnson reflected in her book that it was September 11, more than any other event that led both to deeper US interest and involvement in the Sudanese civil war and greater susceptibility to increased American pressure on the part of the government of Sudan.

---

[8] This potion covers the most part of citation from African union commission inquiry report in which top politicians contributed in information. SPLM members, international organizations, aids workers and other prominent opposition parties' leaders including Dr. Lam Akol was interviewed.

It is the combination of the two that led to the signing of the Comprehensive Peace Agreement (CPA) in 2005. South Sudan was the second new state to be created in the region next to Eritrea. This is where their similarity falls short: whereas Eritrea became independent following the defeat of the government in Ethiopia, "the Derge". The government in Sudan was not defeated by SPLA and they did not win the civil war. The civil war in the Sudan led to an independent in the South following a radically changed international situation following September 11. (Commission of inquiry report).

There is no doubt; wrote the head of UNMISS in her book that September 11th was a factor in bringing the Sudanese government to the negotiating table in a serious way. Rather than the victory in the civil war, SPLA was a beneficiary of an unanticipated change in the international situation. 2005 was the year the SPLA experienced its second major internal political crisis.

On 15th July 2005, Dr. John Garang dissolved the SPLM/A Leadership Council, intending to appoint the new leadership later. It is John Garang's death on 30th July 2005 which averted a full blown political crisis whose dimensions would have been like that in 1991. It is immediately following John Garang's death on 30th July 2005, that Salva Kiir reinstated the dissolved SPLM/A Leadership Council. The Troika became the mainstay of backup support and strategic guidance for parties involved in the negotiations that led to CPA. In her interview with the Commission, Dr. Ann Ito, Acting Secretary-General of SPLM for the past seven years:

credited the Troika with the achievements at Naivasha and the CPA that followed The Troika voluntarily agreed to work together to achieve peace at Naivasha. They agreed to support IGAD, sometimes pressurized them; put funds into all processes of negotiations including workshops and seminars to inform negotiators better. They played a good role in mobilizing funds for implementation of CPA. They helped monitor the process of implementation from 2005 to 2011.

Dr. Lam Akol revealed:

CPA gave SPLM the power it could not have got by political means. It made it possible for SPLM to entrench itself in the agreement. They gave themselves all the power and marginalized everyone else. The state became the SPLM and the SPLM became the state.

He went on to contrast 2005; the year the CPA was signed and the transition began with 1972; the year first civil war ended with the signing of the Addis Ababa Agreement.

The agreement in 1972 was negotiated by a party called SSLM which did not carve out for itself all the power. We had a vibrant but plural power even though there was a single party in Khartoum. But SPLM got power through an agreement not through election. After excluding everyone else, they began to exclude themselves.

The relationship of SPLA to other political forces in South Sudan, no matter how weak, went through a sea change after the referendum. Before the referendum, SPLA was open to any negotiation with internal forces that's their cooperation and support is needed during the process leading to independence. After the referendum, SPLA saw these forces as a handicap to exercising power, a nuisance that could be dispensed, especially given that it could count on firm support from the Troika.

He went on by recalling 2010, the year before the referendum, as the last time SPLM was interested in negotiations with other southern political parties.

The All-South Sudan Political Parties Conference was held in October 2010.

It ended with road map which called for a transitional government of national unity composed of all political parties headed by Salva Kiir, the then de facto President, and included an agreement to hold a Constitutional Conference and another election in two years. Following the referendum, the SPLM Political Bureau met and said they have an electoral mandate and will rule until 2015. They formed a committee and revised the constitution. Really, they formed a committee so they could recycle the provisional constitution as a permanent one. The consensus built in the 2010 was shattered. South Sudan may exist as a state juridical but more as a juridical fiction than an institutional reality. From 2005 to now, there has been no freedom of expression.

The editor on daily monitor shed light on this; he explained that:

> the machinery of the state was never equal to implementing policy, even when it came to repression. There is the tendency of dictatorship but not the capacity for it. The political order created under the CPA was not a dictatorship of a single party, rather a dictatorship of all armed groups. In brief, the Comprehensive Peace Agreement (CPA) was responsible for setting up an unchallenged armed power in South Sudan and thereby legitimizing both anyone holding a gun and the rule of the gun.

The editor of Citizen explained that:

> The problem lay at the top, not with the shortage of trained personnel. There were lots of people attached to each Ministry for the past eight years. But there is no political will to implement what has been recommended. The challenge is with the leadership. If you want to assist us, start correcting people from above. The struggle for liberation united us in the past but there is neither liberation nor vision today.

He concurred:

The international community prepared the ground for the current leadership. The election of Sudan became the legitimating for the government in South Sudan. There was no interim government, no fresh elections. To think of South Sudan as a failed state is to overlook the simple fact that the very political foundation for the existence of a state a political compact has yet to be forged within the elite and between the communities that comprise South Sudan

6.6 The IGAD Mediation Process and Monitoring Mechanism

In South Sudan, IGAD for the second time engaged in south Sudanese conflict which resulted into CPA II. IGAD and her friends (the troika) with Africa union exert endless effort to get out South Sudan from the tribal political plunged civil war. The IGAD mediated peace process funded by international community and the troika tried it's best to deliver meaningful peace in South Sudan. In the first meeting for South Sudan peace talk since the outbreak of war, the reasonable ground was reached by signing cessation of hostility matrix (CoH) on January 23rd, 2014. In this agreement, the government of republic of South Sudan and the armed SPLM/A IO agrees on following:

o To cease all the hostile practice on the date of signing the matrix to open reasonable ground for further dialogue o The parties to conflict agree to get the solution on round table dialogue with help of IGAD head of state and avoid military solution by any mean possible

o Need for full implementation of cessation of hostilities signed on 23rd of January and the subsequence modalities that will be under way some on 24th of January and so on.

Not more than five hours after signing of cessation of hostilities, the armed parties to the conflict violated the agreement and more atrocities was carried out on both sides. This was reported by IGAD monitoring verification team, Human right watch and African union commission of inquiry. Nevertheless, with tireless effort from IGAD head of state and the donors; IGAD friends (the troika), United Nations and international community, the peace process was still going on and the agreement was reached on May 9, 2014. The agreement was about:

o Recognition of no military solution to the crisis in South Sudan, and that a sustainable peace can be achieved only through inclusive political dialogue.
o Understanding the need to take bold decisions in the interest of national reconciliation that can guide the country to a new political dispensation and a permanent constitutional order.

o Recommitment of the parties to immediately cease all hostile activities within twenty-four (24) hours of the signing of this agreement, thus re-dedicating their selves to the Cessation of Hostilities Agreement of 23 January 2014; and further agree to facilitate the full deployment of IGAD Monitoring and Verification Mechanism(MVM).

o Commitment of the armed parties to the conflict to disengage and separate forces and refrain from any provocative action or combat movement until a permanent cease fire is agreed and signed.

o On agreeing to issue, all parties should order all their respective commands and units on signing of the agreement, instructing full and immediate cessation of hostilities, cooperation with the IGAD MVM and facilitation of humanitarian access while the receipt of orders at command level shall be verified by the IGAD MVM in a week after signing this agreement.

o The parties' agreement to open humanitarian corridors in accordance with the Cessation of Hostilities Agreement of 23 January 2014 and the 5 May 2014 [Recommitment on Humanitarian Matters in the CoH Agreement] and to cooperate unconditionally with the UN and humanitarian agencies to ensure that humanitarian aid reaches affected populations in all areas of South Sudan.

o To resolve and to engage in substantive discussions via the IGAD-led peace process on agendas as constituted by the mediation process.

o The agreement that a transitional government of national unity will offer the best chance for the people of South Sudan to take the country forward and that such a government shall oversee government functions during a transitional period, implement critical reforms as negotiated through the peace process, oversee a permanent constitutional process, and guide the country to new elections while direct the warring parties and other stakeholders' respective representatives to the IGAD- led peace process to negotiate the terms of a transitional government of national unity.

o The agreement to ensure the inclusion of all South Sudanese stakeholders in the peace process and the negotiation of a transitional government of national unity to ensure broad ownership of the agreed outcomes. The Stakeholders included the two directly engaged armed parties (the GRSS and the SPLM/A in Opposition), and others such as the SPLM leaders (former detainees), political parties, civil society, and faith-based leaders.

o The agreement on that these other stakeholders shall participate in negotiations on transitional government of national unity, the permanent constitution making committee, and any other items that concern the political future of the country and reconciliation of South Sudanese communities.

o The agreement to fully cooperate with the AU Commission of inquiry and facilitate implementation of its forthcoming recommendations.

o The Agree to meet again within one month under IGAD auspices, to facilitate continued progress on the afore-mentioned issues and resolution of the crisis.

During signature of this agreement, the South Sudanese communities and the helper on peace process sees improved step on the way forward for South Sudan to regain momentum and go up for peace. But a war lord from government side called Gen. Paul Malong Awan, a former Northern Bar el gazel governor who mobilized Mathiang-Anyoor was sworn in as SPLA chief of generals' staff and carried out his Spring campaign which resulted into recapturing of Bentiu, Ayod, Nasir, Longechuk, and all the areas in front of Lou Nuer land including Duk Padiet, Gadiang and others from SPLA IO. This was serious violation which derived a condemnation from UN, IGAD, Troika, international community and the South Sudanese by themselves. On August 25, 2014, the rededication and implementation modalities for cessation of hostilities agreement were signed. In this agreement, the parties to the conflict:

o Acknowledge the needs for full implementation of cessation of hostilities signed on the 23rd of January 2013 and subsequence agreement on the implementation modalities of 24th February 2014, and the recommitment on humanitarian matters signed on 5th of May 2014 and the agreement to resolves the crisis in South Sudan signed on 9th May 2014.

o Regret the numerous violations on cessation of hostilities agreement, the continuous violence and the serious of destruction caused by this violation, while the avoidable loss of lives resulted from this conflict was also regretted.
o Agreed to respect the declared cessation of hostilities, to cease all hostile propaganda in media and to fully guarantee protection of civilians
o Recommitted to declare the position of their forces and to communicate with IGAD monitoring and verification mechanism to insure the implementation of cessation of hostilities agreement is completed without hindrance or delay.
o Recognized the grave threats posed by the humanitarians' situation resulting from this conflict and committed to facilitate full and unhindered humanitarian access to all areas of South Sudan in compliance with an agreement
o Underlined that both parties are abided by national and international laws to prevent recruitment and mobilization of child soldiers and that the recruitment and uses of child soldiers constituted violation and deserve the war crime.

In some occasion, this agreement was respected but violation still raging on and the military confrontation was imminent between warring parties. After this peace agreement, many peace agreements were signed in co-ordination to Addis Ababa IGAD led peace process. In 2015, on August and September respectively, the CPA II and permanent cease fire modal were signed.

What next? The real answer to this question is;

"Its Implementation and restoring South Sudan to be living country".

To oversee the signed peace agreement, IGAD monitoring and verification mechanism was established as an institution that should monitor and verified the warring parties on their violation for agreement. Major General Mohamed of the IGAD Mediation Team explained the operational details of IGAD mediation:

IGAD has eight monitoring teams. There are seven teams in three states; the Upper Nile state, Jonglei state and Unity state, and one mobile team in Juba. The standard strength of a team is six to eight: six internationals, two from each side and three from the community. The protection force is from UNMISS, three battalions. These forces are deploying for protection of civilians (IDPs) as a priority.

6.7 The Emergence of Third Group in Peace Talk

The third group was formed in peace talk; participating as another stakeholder during peace process in Addis Ababa. This was after freeing of the first seven SPLM leaders on custody of Kenyan government. This group was called SPLM leaders and was challenged by many groups, as they were described the betrayers to Dr. Riek Machar. This group was formed due to difference in the interest as well as on how to solve this crisis.

This group claimed that the armed resistance used by Dr. Riek was not their intention because they thought that the arm will still increase the suffering of the communities. But the element from SPLM/ A IO and others organization described this group as the position lobbyer. They were called by Kenyan opposition parties as selfish politicians who ever forgot the cause of their imprisonment and their colleagues who day to day called their unconditional release. These opposition parties called the G10's unconditional push out from Kenyan land.

In fact, G-10 has no difference with Dr. Machar; that was what made them to be denied by some of comrades detained with them since weeks of December. Prof. Peter Adwok Nyaba denied this group during the interview when he reached Addis Ababa for the first time. When asked for which opposition side he wants to joint? He said: I don't know the other opposition group in this conflict because the reform we talked about is what the SPLM/A IO is yearning for and we are the same in opposing the regime of Salva Kiir. Former ambassador, Ezekiel Lol Gatkuoth abandoned the group too for he doesn't see any reasonable ground not to join the SPLM/A IO for they do have the same demand since the December.

Their call for reform is what engulf the country to this conflict; no way to pretend on resisting Salva Kiir. The analysts and the media house claimed that this group was convinced to take over the leadership as Dr. Riek and President Salva Kiir might be forced to move a side. Nevertheless, they said; their plan was an ignorance for military solution and chosen peace to solve this problem.

6.8 The SPLM Re-unification in Arusha

The SPLM re-unification was carried out in Arusha (Tanzania) from January 8-19, 2015, under the auspices of Chama cha Mapinduzi (CCM) chaired by the former vice chairman of CCM John Samuel Malecela and facilitated by the CCM secretary general; Mr. Abdurrahman Kinana. The SPLM reunification was opposed by element from both side especially the top military generals for the sacks of preferring military solution. Some of the opponents counted the SPLM as failed political party which failed to overcome its internal difference within the party and plunged the country into senseless war; some called for its change. The intra-dialogue did not step aside for this call; the parties went on and agree on political issues, organizational issues and on leadership issues. The following are highlight on the agreement.

- Implement and comply with the provisions of cessation of hostilities agreement and use this intra dialogue in Arusha and IGAD peace process in Addis Ababa to expedite the conclusion of the peace agreement to end war.
- SPLM leadership shall make public apology to people of South Sudan for what was happened in December 15, 2013.
- Combating the culture of tribalism, militarism and sectarianism in political life and open space for political environment that promote genuine political pluralism.

- Ensure that the SPLM redefines its ideological direction, developmental path, the nature of its democracy, system of governance and the nature of society and the state it aspire to build.
- Revocation of dismissal of party cadres from party membership and leadership position resulting from the internal conflict within the party
- The SPLM shall uphold principle of accountability, transparence and good governance to combat corruption and malpractice in the party and government.
- Failure to institutionalize and democratize the exercise of power in the party is among the root cause of conflict
- The SPLM general secretariat shall be structured and reorganized to streamlines its offices and function to insure efficiency and effectiveness
- It was agreed that the National Liberation Council (NLC) shall revise and view the contentious provisions, in the drafted SPLM constitution to insure internal democracy within the party.
- The polite bureau (PB) shall develop a party leadership code of conduct and disciplinary procedure to be applicable and upheld by all members irrespective of their position. Both document shall be approved and adopted by national liberation council (NLC).

Many other issues on agreement were not included but the most important points are here. These agreed important points suggested by Tanzanian CCM party, that can benefit everybody in South Sudan were not implemented. They were violated in daylight by bad political ideology pushed by tribalism.

6.9 The Failure of IGAD Mediated Peace Talk

The involvement of IGAD is praised by some groups as it has said to have averted the looming genocide from white army. Nevertheless, the great challenge was that some of the IGAD states only present their self interest in young nation. The Uganda becomes a fighting force alongside government of Salva Kiir being involved in conflict without consensus from head of states convention. The IGAD involvement was said to be good but these same persons called for the departure of Ugandan troops and a reassessment of the role of UNMISS since both were said to be rapidly turning into a hindrance in restoring peace in the country.

Ugandan troops have become a party to the conflict, supporting one side in it. UNMISS too, was seen by some as a partisan force on the side of the IDPs and not the government. Of course, UNMISS may be described as partisan force on side of IDPs because protecting the innocents' civilians right is its mandate, while government by herself is one killing the civilians.

IGAD role was praised by South Sudanese since the last showdown that was made for returning Dr. Riek Machar to Juba city was considered success to IGAD. The suffered population of South Sudan was very happy since they expected that the war has come to an immediate end. Things fall apart in July when Salva Kiir government established some check points which hindered the movement of former first vice president.

In July 2, 2016 prior to check point clashes, the government security force had decided to kill Colonel George Gismalla and captain Domach Koat Pinyien both security operative of SPLA IO. The death of this two SPLA IO comrades fueled the already fragile security situation in Juba and both were only waiting for the trigger to be ignited. Somedays later, the SPLA IO convoy was attacked where their force was over-powered and the belonged pick-up car was seized. Salva Kiir soldiers in Gudele check point have so many times stopped the first vice president convoy going to office to be checked for unknown reasons.

The situation still deteriorating up to July 7 incident in Gudele. It was in evening hour at around 8:00 PM in Gudele check point near Lou clinic where a convoy of SPLA IO who tried to bring food in town for their commander's (first vice president) guards was stopped by government soldiers. When the SPLA IO tried to resist, the government force opened fire at them and in the same manner the SPLA IO opened fire toward the trigger. Thus, the confrontation ended up with two wounded in SPLA IO side and five pronounced dead in government side.

In July 8, the presidency decided to meet to ease the skyrocketing situation which rocked the city in weeks of tension. Nobody knows it was a last showdown on assassination attempt of former first vice president Dr. Riek Machar. While the presidency was in meeting, a disgruntled group came of nowhere entered J1 compound merged-up with president Salva Kiir's body guard and opened fire on first vice president's guard Dr. Riek Machar.

Now! The unjust war and failure of IGAD mediated peace talk started. What made IGAD mediated peace talk fail? IGAD head of state was an imposer and mediator of South Sudan peace process. African Union in coordination with IGAD assigned personnel headed by former Botswana president Fetus Mogea to oversee the implementation process. Since the several attacks and the weeks of tension, IGAD did not intervene to help calm the situation.

After the fight in presidential palace in J1, continues attacks with aerial bombardment in first vice president bases was carried out without single peace guarantor to either intervene, condemn or convince the president to immediately stop that reckless action against peace partner. President Salva Kiir persuaded his peace partner Dr. Riek Machar for forty days up to Congo boarder where he was rescued by UN mission and Congolese authority in Goma National Park of North Kivu province. The copy of persuading letter as of directive from office of the president was furnished to all the offices of deputies' chiefs of Generals staffs, the general headquarters, the office of minister of defense, the office of national security and the air space unit. The letter headed " **C-I-C directives to attack the hideout of Dr. Riek Machar**" was signed by former chief of general staff General Paul Malong Awan and point out the following directives:

- As per the commander in chief (C-I-C) directive, I am hereby directing you to immediately attack and carryout aerial bombardment against the hideout of Dr. Riek Machar, the former first vice president

- You must bring him dead or alive to answer all the charges against him
- You must also make sure that our forces are deployed along South Sudan-DRC border to lay point ambushes against Machar and his force because is heading toward DR Congo. This is for immediate execution he concluded.

After the extraction of Dr. Riek from there, he was airlifted to Khartoum. Now the IGAD become aware of Riek Machar still alive. In this matter, the IGAD's final decision became an isolation policy toward Dr. Riek Machar and forcefully confined him in South Africa. By that end, the IGAD head of state mediated peace talk is assumed luring tactic to kill Dr. Riek in Juba. When they failed, the decision became how to distance him away from his force and president Kiir should crash him militarily.

Now! the peace has dead and the war become an option where president Kiir tried his level best up to the last time when he captures the head quarter of Dr. Riek. Lately, IGAD head of state come up with revitalization forum which risk failure if it should not be given a priority for permanent peaceful settlement.

6.10 Dr. Riek's Relentless Pursuant for Peace to Held in South Sudan

Dr. Riek Machar Teny Dhurgon, a political scientist and a known prominent politician in political arena of South Sudan since his joining SPLM/SPLA in 1984, became the center of political domination in South Sudan. Dr. Riek, who defected from SPLM /A main stream and formed his own movement in 1991, accused Dr. John Garang of lacking fruit of democracy. He signed many peace agreements with Sudan supported by most of the western nations for South Sudanese to have their own self-determined country. Since the historic Nasir declaration of August 28, 1991, the demand of people of South Sudan for the right to self-determination as a peaceful political resolution of the forty years' war in Sudan has been a real challenging problem to Sudanese political forces and parties.

The SSIM/A had been engaged in many peace initiatives with the regime of National Islamic front (NIF) to find a solution to the conflict. Among these initiatives were: Frankfurt peace talk of January 25, 1992, the Nigerian mediated Abuja peace talks of May/June 1992, the Nairobi May/June 1993 talks and intergovernmental authority on drought and development (IGADD), January 6th, 1994 through September 19, 1994 peace talk, Khartoum peace agreement in 1997 and many others agreement which included Washington declaration etc.

In these talks, the SSIM/A had demonstrated its commitment to the search for the lasting and just peace in South Sudan and above all the SSIM/A had specifically underlined the right of self-determination for the people of South Sudan as the cornerstone for settlement that would meet their legitimate aspiration. Dr. Riek who stated that the humiliation from North could end up when independent South Sudan is acquired, was opposed by many politicians of SPLM/A, some of them from his tribe.

Due to Dr. Riek's wishes for permanent peace, he concluded his campaign of self-determination and rejoined the SPLM/A in 2002 with full confident of South Sudan to be independent country. Dr. Riek managed to convince Dr. John Garang and accepted the self-determination as an objective to fight for, instead of unity for whole Sudan which led them into split. Dr. Riek also mediated the former chairman and co-founder of SPLM/A, and his commander currently the South Sudan president, Salva Kiir Mayardit in 2004. Also through 2013 South Sudanese civil war, Dr. Riek played the following role.

- In January 2014, Dr. Riek again accepted to negotiate with Salva Kiir who massacred his tribe in eye of everyone in South Sudan believing the peace as solution to every disagreement.

- During the peace process, Dr. Riek agreed to be served under his own rival as vice president for finding the solution to end the conflict. Now! The peace has been signed; he accepted to return to South Sudan and President Salva Kiir still's president.

- As of beginning of 2016, he flied to Uganda which has been a party to the conflict fighting alongside his rival force. Uganda pledged to capture Dr. Riek within three days in the first week of conflict in 2014 but failed to do so as of harsh resistance from opposition army. Is it not searching for permanent peace in South Sudan?

- But in unexpected move, another war broke out in J1 "the palace". This was where his supporters, analysts and some observers says; the IGAD-plus imposed peace initiative was a luring tactic from President Salva Kiir and his friends from peace granting partners to assassinate Dr. Riek Machar in capital Juba.

- Thus, Dr. Riek was chased away from Juba being persuaded in bush for forty days without anyone from peace granting partners to pick him up or stop the president Salva persuading his peace partner.

As of this matter, Dr. Riek still only calls for permanent peace and resuscitation of August 2015 peace agreement after he was rescued by UN mission in Congo. Is this not a permanent search for peace? His calls for peace after staying in bush for forty days angered some of his comrades in which his former minister Ramadan Hassen Laku was the first man claiming that justice will not prevail under Machar's leadership. Let alone the above circumstance, Dr. Riek Machar Teny Dhurgon was forcefully confined by US-led IGAD policy of isolation in South Africa. Dr. Riek also days by days is calling for the way to find permanent peace in South Sudan and calling for non-interested party initiative for permanent solution to conflict.

To conclude his pursuant for peace: Dr. Riek felt into many conflicts with his tribe for blame on his acceptance for peace which his ethnic politicians see as none profitable. Drawback to Khartoum peace agreement in 1997, Dr. Riek disagrees with some of his senior commanders in SSIM/A for signing what they termed as unjust peace. He also falls out with many of his comrades on idea of his return to bush and to negotiate with their rival in SPLM/A. The disagreement on the issue of returning to bush to be merge with SPLA under John Garang was what led Riek Gai Kok and Elijah Hon Top to serve under Khartoum government where Elijah Hon face his sudden death in hand of Arab led government.

The same Nairobi re-unification initiative in 2002 which did not treat the SSIM/A element in way they expected, was what resulted into defection of high ranking commander; late General Tito Biel Chuor and some comrades, and rejoined Khartoum government. The same disagreement re-occurred in SPLM/A IO.

Dr. Riek's love for peace more than his party supporters' expectation was what resulted into defection of his powerful generals who initiated the rebellion in which general Peter Gatdet, Gat-hoth Gatkuoth, late Gabriel Tang-Giny, John Chuol Gakah and others high ranking generals were among the defectors. Those defected generals who talked loudly not to have any peace agreement that maintain Salva Kiir president of the republic of South Sudan and the rejection of SPLM re-unification, calls for SPLM/A to be renamed, as the name indicated Sudan liberation not South Sudan and demanded the name to be reformed into South Sudan army.

These generals were blaming Dr. Riek for what they have described as negligence on military solution to the conflict and failure to arm the army and fight the confused tribal war. In statement from generals', reasons for their defection were stated as follow. During SPLM/A IO general meeting on April 15-18, 2014 in Nasir, the declaration of movement and endorsement of Riek to be its leader and the intension to wage war and overthrow Salva militarily was discussed. In the second meeting of December 2015 in Pagak, the following resolution was adopted.

- o Rejection of any peace agreement that maintain Salva Kiir the president of South Sudan
- o Acceptance of bringing the ammunition and others army facilities
- o Accept any peace agreement that make Dr. Riek prime minister of the country
- o Adoption of federalism and democratic structure

- o Call for Salva Kiir to resign and others important point.

The 3rd meeting also conducted in Pagak was a revision of all the above resolution and some new issues concerning the movement. All this resolution was violated by Riek himself and signed the agreement on his own will. This was what led to their defection, "they have stated". Other top politicians including professor De-Chand, Gabriel Changson Lew Chang and others from his tribe blamed Dr. Riek for the same above-mentioned claims from generals and defected too.

All in all, the author describes Dr. Riek as a peace-loving element in addition to other citizens who are in support of search for permanent peace when the country is in dire need of it. Now the CPA II mediated by head of the state is signed but the bad political ideology still pulling back the country where the second war re-erupted in July 8, 2016. If its implementation process should have been follow carefully, peace may return to South Sudan.

[9] **Chapter Seven**

What to Be Done for the Restoration of Young Nation

As a sum-up, on the above discussed topics, the South Sudanese let alone leaders need a lot of task to engages in for restoration of harmony in young nation. What the South Sudanese expected since the end of Sudanese civil war in 2005, is not found nowadays in young nation. Though, to restore this expectation and for South Sudanese to get back to day one, as to believe co-existence a tool to peaceful living, the responsibility must be carry out by every citizen.

The leaders of South Sudan need to bring back the peace they have stolen and apologize to the nations, then the process of peaceful living should be practice. The people of South Sudan needs reconciliation among them that can be carry out by every citizen. The young nation has been badly affects by current war; break it down into tribal nation and became failed state.

---

[9] The young nation's leaders need to be abided by peace agreement and carry out work of restoration in New Transitional Government of National Unity, where all other stakeholder from the entire country should participate. The people of South Sudan needs to be teaches with forgiveness and toleration as these are the tools for peaceful living

Nevertheless, the people of South Sudan did not cease ambition and call to live together.

- o The cases happened when some Nuer individuals still living in Warrap and Wau and got not killed by the Dinka community.
- o The same was true when the Dinka were transported from Pagak, Maiwut and other areas in Upper Nile through Ethiopian border since outbreak of war.
- o The same case was when Chol Aruei, a high profiled officer from SPLM IG and other officials from Dinka were captured by Nuer in Fangak. These top politicians were kept in good conditions and prepared a farewell for them when released while heading to Juba, the heart of government.

These are some good examples which show that South Sudanese are being engaged against each other by the leadership not the communities themselves. The South Sudanese needs to reconcile and this reconciliation can be taken through many channels like the following.

7.1 Political Tolerance

Political tolerance is started with political socialization. Political socialization means a process where every citizen, politicians whether in ruling party or opposition parties develop the values, attitudes, beliefs, and opinions that enable them to support the political system. It is also a kind of behaving in accordance with rules, norms and expectation of one's own state and society.

As a country leaders who respect their legitimacy, leaders cannot afford to ignore the way of its citizens develop their political view. South Sudanese needs to understand political toleration not only between politicians. The leaders of South Sudan let alone the members of SPLM in young nation, needs to task themselves with political toleration. The politicians around the globe are those who cause day to day mess of the nations. But the tools used by wise leaders are the ways of possible and peaceful understanding for the sacks of country and its people. The author is very optimistic without question on supporting the idea that South Sudanese communities did not cease their demand to live in peaceful state as brothers and sisters, mother and fathers, elders and oldies. But the leaders' failure to adhere to fruit of democracy is the main problem that plunged the country into current mess.

A true measure of political system is the kind of citizen it produces (Aristotle). In a democratic philosophy, a good state is the one whose model citizen is also good person. A bad state is a one whose model citizen obeys order without regard to question of good or evil. The fact is that civic virtue cannot be divorced from personal integrity. In general, it is agreed that good citizen is made not born. The political toleration between politicians will let them understand each other and give a solution to any obstacle. It would also pave the way to create good citizen. Every human being is selfish born with jealous and ignorance. That is only in some stages where individuals' external intelligence helps the persons in ways he/she can behave. Living in harmony with different nationalities and tolerating each other is the key to peaceful co-existence.

Toleration would also erase tribal hatred toward each other and the state of patriotism should be adopted, though the ideas that cause communities division could be avoid.

7.2 Fuller Understanding of Fruit of Democracy

Fruit of democracy start up with strong political leadership where political toleration, patriotism, responsibilities and accountability are the vital role to it is accomplishment. But the main case here is for nations' leaders to place in front the nationwide interest. The nations' interests are the way to peaceful co-existence when respected. Starting from rights of individual both as human being and through democratic process (human and democratic right) should be respected.

The leaders of this young nation need to consider that ''the human is a free agent with inherent right based on promise that all are ultimately equal in power, freedom and in their desire for self-reservation''. The nation interest needs to be put in front of everyone to facilitate peaceful living among the nations. Putting in front the nation interest is another way of solving problems and is a solution. And this process should be carryout by showing strong political leadership.

7.2.1 Strong Political Leadership

The well-being of nations often depends on the capacity of leaders to choose wisely and act prudently. Per one eminent scholar, politics is a leadership or attempted leadership of whatever is the prevailing form of political community. Every community and country is profoundly affected by the quality of its political leadership. There are four types of leadership.

Demagogues' leader: deceive and manipulate the people for selfish ends. They are schemers, rabble-rousers and warmongers

Ordinary politicians: do no great harm or good and concentrate above all on getting re-elected

Citizen leader: hold no official public office but become actively involved in and can significantly influence a nation's politics

True leaders: are political architects who create new states which is change in political ideology. They are the peace maker who resolves conflicts and the orators who inspire in time of national crisis. They are the yesterday's founder, today's path finder and tomorrow's legend. True leaders always practice state craft (wise use of state power). Statesmanship (gifted leader) is leaders who make a lasting difference which are termed as a men and women of rare quality.

A leader must to be statesmanship where they display a firm commitment to peace, harmony and public goods that possesses extra political skill and exhibit practical wisdom in time of crisis. These men and women provide crucial leadership necessary for the nation's survival.

Strong political leadership is show by the leaders' commitment in maintaining peaceful co-existence and conflict resolution mechanism. One typical habit in conflict resolution is to give up in very high priority on defending one's own interest. The leaders of the nation are expected to defend the national interest and to defeat the interest of one self-claimed interests. In any circumstance, parties to the conflict are usually inclined to see their interests as diametrically opposed. The possible outcomes are seen to be win-lose or win-win (compromise). But be assure that there is much more common outcome in violence conflict; both lose if neither can impose an outcome or prepared to compromise and win-lose (one party win, other lose) if either can impose an outcome or is prepared to compromise.

In conflict resolution analysis, this is found to be much more common outcome that is generally supposed. When this become clear to the parties, there is strong motive based on little move out of self-interest for moving toward other outcome such as compromise or win-win. The better course that the true leaders do is to persuade the people that the pursuit of public interest is in everyone's interest and that the private interest not and ought not to be the primary concern of public policy. A true leader is motivated by neither cross self-interest nor narrow partisanship but by consideration of the non-partisan public good or the general welfare and such leader acquire popularity. Such a decision is possible only in mind that is detached from the agitation of moment as well as the insight which come from an objective and discerning knowledge of the facts. The true leader must have a political wisdom.

This wisdom must possess prudent practical wisdom "Aristotle". A compelling vision of public goods is useless without way of achieving it. A true leader understands the relationship between immediate action and ultimate consequence. They can distinguish between the enduring and the ephemeral, the fundamental and the frivolous, the possible and unattainable. In sum, statesman requires rare insight and ability to both diagnose problem and prescribes remedies. Wise leader bears a resemblance for good should the community proceed.

Having a national interest as a slogan as well as reconciling wisdom and consent in the often-turbulent public arena, is one of the primary tasks of leadership in a democracy. A leader must be able to manage a vast bureaucracy and direct a large personnel staff to work with the legislature and mature passage of administrative program. This is to rally public opinion behind policies and that is what we call political skill. Political wisdom presupposes that the requisite leadership skill is put to good and proper use. Any political leader who seeks to remove obstacle to needed social reform by ruining, jailing or killing the opponents can hardly be praised for his/her actions, no matter how beneficial their policies maybe.

The result is loss for their popularity and creating more enemies. The cores of all good leadership are elusive qualities such as intuition, inspiration and good judgement. 'Politician doesn't mean leader" a politician and real leader have great different. Great leader cannot ignore special interest but it happens that all leaders may act like politicians.

A politician begins to act like a leader whenever he or she stops trying merely to testify the momentary of constituents. Most politicians work only for a partial interest which most of the time result in to themselves. The South Sudanese leaders' needs to restraint from acting as politicians instead, they need to adopt the fruit of good leadership. This would be the only possible mean to help rescue those suffering poor citizens displaced internally and across the regional borders. Second to that is to carry out the old mean of solving problem. This mean was used to be carried out by traditional-chief, sectional clans war leaders and the elders of respective communities. Comparing to status, we can call this as traditional reconciliation.

7.3 Traditional Reconciliation

Traditionally, the task of conflict resolution has been a helping party who perceive their situation as zero-sum (self-gain and others lose). In this situation, the assistance for other parties to move in positive sum direction is maintained. Long time ago, villagers fight on ethnicity for the case of grazing ground and other issues. These conflicts were solved traditionally on direction from traditional chief and elders. For example: the war between Guek Ngundeng and Deng Malual along-side Kolang Jiarkuach was solved traditionally after the Fangak Nuer bylaw was drafted. When Kolang discovered that Nuer are respectful when you recognize them, he starts to come up with strategy that led to traditional peaceful settlement between this two tribe. The name Turuk Deng Malual left in Nuer community as a ''said word'' from generation to generation by simply showing the event.

The formed TGoNU when come into function, needs to carry out this responsibility. To mobilize elders and traditional chiefs from different tribes and the process of traditional reconciliation should be used. In South Sudan culture, the word from elders and traditional chiefs are the most respected in village, though the traditional reconciliation is more needed. This should be the only possible way to rescue the nations!

Bibliography

Prof. Kinfe Abraham (2005) Sudan, the politic of war and peace; Addis Ababa Ethiopia

Human Right Watch (2014) South Sudan's New War; USA

Human Right Watch (2005) Sudan, Oil and human right; New York USA

US policy to end Sudan's War (2003); New York

The Sudan Democratic Gazette (2002); Sudan

Huge mail, Oliver, Tom (1999) contemporary conflict resolution Cambridge; UK

Steven J (2004) Political Development and Democratic theory; New Delhi

Report on African Union commission of Inquiry on South Sudan crime (2015); Addis Ababa Ethiopia

Report on UNMISS Human Right Department 2014, 2015 and 2016; South Sudan

Kidist Mulugeta (2009) The Role of IGAD and International organization in Resolving the Somalia conflict; Addis Ababa

Mahboub Maalim (2013) IGAD'S Role in Stability and Diplomacy in Horn of Africa; London

Chama Cha Mapinduzi (2015) Agreement on the Reunification of SPLM; Arusha Tanzania

IGAD (2014) Agreement to Resolves the Crisis in South Sudan; Addis Ababa Ethiopia

IGAD (2014) Re-dedication and Implementation Modalities for Cessation of Hostilities Agreement; Addis Ababa Ethiopia

Chama Cha Mapinduzi (2015) The Arusha communiqué; SPLM Intra-Dialogue; Arusha Tanzania

Norman Vierra (1998) Civil Right 3rd edition; MN, USA

Thomas M. PhD (2003) Understanding Politics; USA